In the Frame

hinder Kempter.

Bahé DSho

Caroline Pitcher

In the Frame

Edited by Rowena Edlin-White

Contributors
David Belbin
Pauline Chandler
Berlie Doherty
Gwen Grant
Sylvia Hall
Linda Kempton
Chris d'Lacey
B.K. Mahal
Nick Manns
Lynne Markham
Bette Paul
Caroline Pitcher
Gill Vickery

www.fiveleaves.co.uk

In the Frame

Published in 2006 by Five Leaves
PO Box 8786, Nottingham NG1 9AW
info@fiveleaves.co.uk
www.fiveleaves.co.uk

Five Leaves acknowledges financial assistance
from the Arts Council England

ISBN 1905512090

Cover illustration: David Wyatt

Design and layout by
Four Sheets Design & Print Ltd

Printed and bound in Great Britain

Contents

Introduction

In the Frame is a "baker's dozen" — thirteen stories by thirteen excellent writers for young people, many of whose names I am sure you will recognise. All of them live and work in Nottinghamshire, Derbyshire or Leicestershire and represent only a fraction of the many talented writers in this area.

The stories are all very different but with a common theme: that moment in our lives when we step out of the dependency of childhood and into an adult world where we are expected to be responsible, independent, and make decisions which will affect the rest of our lives; the moment we become aware of ourselves as people with choices and aspirations.

All the main characters in these stories have reached this point in their lives — some much too young — and have suddenly found themselves caught "in the frame", centre stage, sometimes in circumstances beyond their control. The authors have explored how they might react: some rise to the challenge, some are defeated by it; some break out and rebel against the expectations of their family or community; some discover hidden strengths and ways of holding their own in a hostile environment; and some are inspired and propelled into an unexpected future.

The authors were not asked to set their stories in the areas where they live, but I think the influence of the Midlands landscape and history can be detected in many of them. The stories are not all set in the present time: we have contemporary school stories, but also stories set fifty years ago and much further back in history; time-slip stories, fantasy, romance, the supernatural, a murder mystery — something of everything!

These thirteen authors are some of the finest writing for young people anywhere in the UK. I hope you will find some old favourites and discover some new ones "In the Frame".

In the Frame is one of a set of books published to celebrate Five Leaves' tenth birthday. The others are *Sunday Night and Monday Morning*, a collection of fiction by Nottingham authors, and a book of poetry by fifty-three local writers, *Poetry: the Nottingham Collection*.

Rowena Edlin-White
January 2006

Drive
Chris d'Lacey

The first thing Alan Dinwood said to me was: "Oi, do you fancy going for a ride?"

Talk about subtle. Fair enough, the guy was a number one looker. Eyes that would probably glow in the dark and a mouth that had 'drool here' written all over it. But me, I like a bit of charm in my men. A peck of romance. Some sharp conversation. Was I going for a ride! Jeez, what did he think I *was*?

Then Shelley pipes up: "Come on, Lori, you'll love it." Which began to make me wonder about the sort of company I'd got myself into. I'd only moved to Clayborough a couple of months before. Shelley Masson was the first good friend I'd made. She was lively, outgoing, chewed gum all the time. She had promised me a tour of the local talent. And this was the pinnacle: Alan Dinwood, aka Aladdin.

"Why do you call him—?"

"You'll see," Shelley said with a 'trust me' look I didn't trust at all. It made me wonder how many 'rides' she'd been on in the past. I told Shelley straight: I didn't want to be a donkey on Dinwood's beach.

"Chill out," she said. "He's totally ace."

"Oi!" barked Aladdin. Such command of English. "When you two skirts have finished gassing, p'raps we can sort out a time for tonight?"

I faced him squarely. "I haven't said I'll go anywhere with you *yet*."

He looked me up and down and stuck his tongue in his cheek. "Your loss," he said, and gave a quick shrug.

"She'll be there," Shelley piped.

"Shel-*ley*," I whispered, gritting my teeth. "The bloke's a creep. Anyway, I'd have to check it's okay with my dad."

"Eight," said Shelley, ignoring me completely. "At Weenie's Café. Will you be picking us up in the motor or what?"

Dinwood stuck his fists in his left weave jeans. "Nah," he said, "let's take Lori for a walk round, shall we?"

Shelley popped a bubble. "Brilliant," she said.

"Round where?" I put in.

"Just round," said Aladdin.

I don't see a lot of my dad. He got lonely after Mum went. Took refuge in his work. Graphic design. High-powered computers. Our house is positively buzzing with the things. Dad's on some sort of government project. Nothing deep. He's no Alex Rider. Something to do with 'Community Planning', whatever that means. I leave him to it. Don't get involved. Give him a cuddle when he's looking tired. Cook him something, leave it by the screens. I don't have to ask his permission for dates, but telling him is one way of saying I love him.

"I'm out tonight," I told him, massaging his shoulders, "with Shelley — and a guy called Alan Dinwood."

Dad rattled off some keystrokes. The screen in front of us dissolved into a grid. The grid folded in, morphing into a wiry 3D array. Roads and buildings. That kind of thing.

"Anything special?"

"Just walking. Y'know."

He patted my hand. "Glad you're making friends." Then he was back at the keyboard again.

"This a game?" I asked, as the screen zoomed in and we travelled round the buildings like a fly-by camera.

Dad reached for the mouse. "No, it's just work." He dropped a menu and selected 'Full Enhance'. The grid filled with a palette of incredible graphics. Vivid. Life-like. Leaves drifting on a virtual breeze. Birds fighting for bread on a pavement. A young kid wobbling off his bike. Paint by electronic numbers. Wow.

"Whatever you're doing, you're a genius," I told him, and placed a gentle kiss on the top of his head.

"You're a sweet child," he told me in return. "Have a good time. Don't be too late, eh?"

I met Shelley at Weenie's at ten to eight. We had a cappuccino and waited for Aladdin. I hadn't dolled up. Jeans, crop top, black cotton jacket. Casual, like Shelley. We looked all right.

He was fifteen minutes late. He hadn't bothered to change. He turned up with a pal who looked unwashed, unshaven, unamiable. Un-everything.

"That's Gaff," said Shelley, making a move.

"Yeah," I muttered. "I've met his brother, Naff." I left the froth on the coffee and hurried on after her.

We walked around, with Dinwood leading. No big plan. Little conversation. We paced the streets, kicking up autumn leaves. I crossed my arms and followed the great Aladdin, always keeping one pace behind. Gaff and Shelley linked arms, swayed. They fell into doorways, giggling like kids. Alan Dinwood didn't make a move on me. Some 'date' this was. Some dumb ride. That made me think about what Shelley had said, about Dinwood picking us up in his motor. So I made an effort.

"What kind of car have you got, then?" I asked.

Dinwood clicked his tongue and looked over his shoulder. "What kind do you want?" he asked.

I thought, Oh yeah, now it's Mastermind, is it? "Pass," I said.

11

He looked at me gone out. "She ain't told you, has she?"

'She ain't told me.' The guy was a Neanderthal. "She ain't told me what?" I said.

"Hey, Alan," Gaff shouted, releasing the tension, "when are you going to go for some wheels?"

Aladdin looked around. I saw his gaze fasten on a sleek black car on the opposite side of the road. I didn't know the make. Something glossy, like a Porsche. Tinted windows. Pop-up headlights. Big tail fins. Very expensive.

"Wow!" exclaimed Shelley, as Alan crossed the road and paced around the car. "Is that the *Batmobile* or what? Does it fly, d'you think?"

"Has it got a back seat?" Gaff said crudely. He gave Shelley a squeeze and made her yelp.

"Shut up," said Dinwood, "I'm working here."

Then I understood — all that about the 'ride'. My heart skipped a beat. I backed off a pace.

"Oh, no," I said, waving my hands. "I'm not getting wound up in this."

"Who *is* she?" Gaff the unshaven asked Shelley.

"Come on, Lori," Shelley pleaded. She pushed Gaff away. "It's nothing serious. We just bomb round a bit and bring the car back. It's dead exciting. You'll love it. Honest."

"No way," I said again. I was thinking of my dad.

And that's when Shelley saw something weird. "Look at this!" she cried. "You've gotta come *now*!" She pointed to the lettering on the rear of the car: Lorelei.

"I never seen one of these before," said Gaff.

"Sussed you," said a voice. Everyone looked at Alan Aladdin Dinwood. "Open sezame," he said with a grin. Two gull wings lifted on the Lorelei. Even I gasped. You had to say this for the good-looking creep: he knew his stuff. No bent metal. No alarms. No surprises. Open sezahim. Bingo.

"Get in," said Dinwood, sliding into the driver's seat.

"I'm in the front," Gaff said, running.

"Cheers," Shelley snorted. She looked at me. "Oh, come on, Lori, live a little." She tugged me down and into the car.

The door wings closed with a satisfying clunk. I could see Alan Dinwood at work already. He looked puzzled. I knew he was trying to hot wire the ignition. But there *was* no ignition. No wires to hot.

"Let's go," said Shelley, bouncing her ass on the beige leather seat.

"Don't push me," said Dinwood.

"This is crazy," I said. My shoulders felt weak with fear.

"Man, this is one smart car," Gaff whistled. He pressed a button on a pad beside his seat. A panel on the dashboard slid sweetly open.

"Wow, beam me up!" Shelley rattled as the panel revealed a bank of switches.

"Don't touch it!" Aladdin gripped Gaff's arm. He leaned over and studied the bank. His finger hovered, then he hit a button. *You have voice control*, a woman's voice announced.

"Voice control?" I gasped. What kind of car ran on voice control?

"Oh ma-an!" exclaimed Gaff. He beat his fists together like a six year-old.

"Who *was* that?" Shelley asked, frowning, y'know, like three's a crowd.

"Quiet!" barked Dinwood. "Let me think." He gripped the steering wheel and stared at the dash. Options flashed across the LCD screen. Top of the list was the word 'Drive'. Dinwood tried it. "Drive," he grunted. There was a whirring sound. Shelley Masson whooped. Gaff said, "Awesome." Alan said, "Cool." I said nothing. Nothing at all. I just held my breath.

The Lorelei drove.

There was an odd weightless feel about the car. It rose like a Hovercraft. Smoother than chocolate. We pulled away down Tooley Street, took a sharp left into Carver Road.

"Steering's light," Alan Dinwood muttered.

Gaff and Shelley didn't hear. Couldn't care less. They were shrieking like brats on a roller-coaster ride. I was looking for a seat belt. But there *were* no belts. No door catches, either. I was trapped inside the Lorelei. Trapped and scared.

Then Shelley yammered: "Faster!" — and the nightmare began.

Increase speed, the woman's voice said.

"No!" said Dinwood. "Not down here!" We were speeding down a narrow road of terraced houses. There was barely room for a sheet of paper between the sides of the Lorelei and the rows of parked cars.

"Bit close," said Gaff, suddenly getting twitchy.

"Shut it," said Dinwood, hands stiff on the wheel.

"Go into Baker's Road!" said Shelley. "You can cut into the dual carriageway from there!"

The Baker's Road junction flashed towards us.

"Red light," said Gaff.

"No brakes," muttered Dinwood. He banged the wheel. "Brake!" he cried.

The Lorelei sped on.

"What are you doing?" Shelley squealed. She looked back across her shoulder, mouth dropping open. The car was through the light. Somewhere to our left there was a screech of rubber.

"I'm not doing anything!" Dinwood yelled.

"Look out for the roadworks!" Gaff cried out. He put his arm across his face. Shelley screamed. Half a dozen cones sprayed up into the air. Somewhere in the distance a siren sounded.

Shelley yelled, "I want to get out of this car!"

"I can't control it!" Dinwood bellowed.

Then we saw the Pelican crossing. A woman with a pram and a little girl. "No!" shouted Gaff. "Don't cross! Don't cross!" I could hear him scrabbling, kicking back into his seat. The siren grew louder. Shelley screamed again. I clamped my hands and whispered, "Dad." The woman and the little girl looked our way. Horror-stricken faces zoomed towards us. Aladdin pulled down on the steering wheel.

There was a thud. The Lorelei banked and the front end lifted. Shelley was right: the thing could fly. A strange kind of silence gripped us inside. Outside, we saw the world tumbling and rolling. We twisted through the air like a leaping dolphin. We rose to a peak and we waited for the splash.

But the splash didn't come. The door wings lifted and light flooded in.

"Uh?" went Gaff. "Uh, what's this?"

We were still in Tooley Street. The car hadn't moved.

Shelley had her face in her hands by now. She was shouting hysterically. "Am I dead? Am I dead?"

A man in a black peaked cap looked in. "No," he said. "You're under arrest."

A government project. Now I knew. Should have guessed he'd name it after me. His darling daughter. His apple. His Lorelei. He'd always wanted to call me that, he said. But Mum wouldn't have it. She'd haggled for Lori. Beat him down. She was good at that.

They gave me a caution. Gaff and Shelley, too. But it

was nothing compared to the sentence from Dad. Something emptied inside him that day. Part of us really did die in that car. I tried to shift the blame to Alan Roger Dinwood. No way, girl. It was never going to wash. I could see it in his eyes. Shame. Disappointment. Hard crosses for a parent to bear.

The mastermind got six months inside. Four, if he pleased Her Majesty. Yeah. I sometimes wonder, when I think of him there, if he ever gets that pantomime feeling still. I dream of him at nights, pacing his cell. He stops by the steel bars, studying the lock. "Open sezame," he says, with a grin.

Not this time, Aladdin.

Not this time.

In the Frame
Nick Manns

"And now we come to the highlight of the evening, the Victor Snellgrove Prize for creative writing. For those of you who haven't been here before, the Snellgrove Prize, which is worth £250, is awarded each year to the student who has produced the most imaginative piece of work during his — or her — English classes. The late Victor Snellgrove said, and I quote: 'The house of literature contains many rooms. The prize I bequeath to the school is for the most interesting writing produced by any pupil, from Year Seven upwards.' Traditionally the award has been judged by the Head of English, and this year Mr Hardwick has spent long hours weighing up the merits of the various candidates. And so, it gives me great pleasure to ask the Mayor of Gretford, Mrs Cynthia Nolan, to open the envelope and reveal the lucky — or should I say, talented — winner."

(Applause).

I can just see it, can't you, Mr Hardwick? The Head moves to one side; there's wild clapping from the packed school hall and Mrs Nolan steps forward, hair like twisted candy floss and a smile the size of Niagara. She takes the pale cream envelope and looks up at the raked seating. "Exciting, isn't it?" she says, running her finger along the seam, a diamond catching one of the spotlights.

But — even as she's about to reveal the slip of paper to the silent audience; as parents and the press look through their viewfinders and the videotape starts to roll — let's not get ahead of ourselves. Let's sit back and imagine whose name might be scrawled on that cheque. After all, prize-giving isn't until November and we haven't finished this academic year yet. And there's work to be done — as you like to put it. So, let's leave everyone away in the future, sitting under those soft orange lights, and think about where we are now. And what we have to do.

I mean, for me, it's pretty straightforward, Mr Hardwick. Here I am, bent over this table in a poky little office to the left of Reception. I have a grey filing cabinet, a metal wastepaper bin and the remains of a dried up plant for company. Through the window — which is all of two and half metres away — I can see the pale brick and flat roof of the DT block. And if I move my head back a bit, I can see the plate glass window of the dining hall, the flower bed a mass of crisp packets and chocolate wrappers, glistening in the light spring rain.

And in front of me? An A4 sheet of questions for my mock English Language paper. About as exciting as a fast-food menu.

But don't let's get too long-faced. I mean, hand on heart, I quite like this opportunity to express myself, without interruption. Question four reads: 'Write a review of some performance that you've witnessed'. Well, that leaves a lot of scope for the imagination, Mr Hardwick.

Performance? Mr Forester, next door, was an Oscar nominee when the police came to drag him away for battering Mrs Forester on New Year's Eve. And Suzanne Cooper, in the lock-up at the back of the fire station last summer, has to be some kind of medal contender.

Anyhow, let's take a slow walk down Memory Lane: look back on another performance; spot the actors with star quality.

As you know, I have taken the occasional Thursday off school. Not to lie in bed and think of England, but to get up early, load the van and help my poor old mum down the market. She's had this odds and sods stall for about five years, and we're set up and ready to go by 7am most mornings. Although I have 'seriously jeopardised' my education et cetera by playing truant, I've tried to help the old dear out. Single parent and all that. As I see it, I get a bit of work experience and the family business struggles on.

This particular day, I'm sitting on my stool, sipping tea, and I'm aware — out of the corner of my eye — that I have a punter. So, I looks up from the paper and I'm staring right into the eyes of my English teacher (let's call him Mr Hardwick).

"What do you think you're doing?" he asks.

And for a minute I thought I hadn't heard him quite right. What does it look like I'm doing, I want to say, painting the Mona Lisa? But I keep my big trap shut and stop reading about Lucinda Bianci's failed boob-job.

At this point, of course, Mum trundles up, sees me staring like an idiot, and tries to be helpful: "Anything take your fancy, dear?" she says, gesturing with her arms.

"Mum—" I start to say, but am interrupted when Mr Hardwick puts down his briefcase and says, "Are you this boy's mother?" All serious, with eyebrows pinched together like a retarded whippet.

"Yes," says Mum, and I can see that she's trying to place the face, make sense of the situation.

"Well," says Mr H, adjusting the knot of his tie, "he should be in school." He looks down at his watch. "In fact, he should be in Maths at this moment. He has GCSE exams in three months' time."

"Oh," says Mum, stretching her mouth like she's playing Jack's mother in a Christmas panto. "Steven, you naughty boy. You said you was on study leave."

I feel I should say, "But I've got these magic beans, Mother," but I'm stopped by the 'awkward silence' that opens up — like we're all struck dumb because nobody knows whose turn it is. Like you expect someone from the side to read out the next line.

"And that's not all," says the stoat-faced teacher, eventually. "Many of the books on sale here come from Gretford High School."

He pauses, as if waiting for us both to keel over and start jerking, but instead, Mum stops wiping her hands across her apron and leans forward.

"I don't know anything about that, Mister," she says. "We buy and sell all the time. Can't go round checking everything —"

"Mrs Sullivan, there's half a class set of *Wind in the Willows* right in front of you, and various editions of Shakespeare plays, all prominently marked with the Gretford school stamp. Some of them are brand new — delivered to the school less than six months ago."

"Well," she says. "Can't say we've been shifting many — cluttering up the place, if you ask me. What do you say, Stevie?"

I'm still recovering from the shock of seeing Hardwick standing there, so all I can come out with is, "Yer."

Mind you, I can see that the big man is beginning to get annoyed with how everything is turning out. There's a touch of colour in his cheeks and he pushes up his black specs in irritation.

"This is all beside the point, Mrs Sullivan —"

"But excuse me," comes back Mum, "you've been making all these accusations about Stevie and myself.

About his skiving school and us receiving and selling stolen goods — who are you, when you're at home?"

Well, you know how it all ended, Mr Hardwick. We shovel all the offensive items into a couple of boxes and I accompany you back to the College of Knowledge. And the very next thing, after I've spent the best part of the day hanging around the Head's door, is that I'm given an 'indefinite suspension' and have to take my mock exams in a room the size of a garden shed.

So. Where do we go from here? And, more to the point, how can we help one another?

"I beg your pardon?" I hear you say, suddenly waking up for the first time in your weekend chore of ticking exam papers.

The thing is, Mr Hardwick, I'm not that excited about my current situation. I've had to put up with the humiliation of being parted from the comfort and support of my peers (Daz was especially narked by my absence from Friday afternoon Science) and I don't think my current circumstances will impress anyone when I parade for interview at Gretford College next August.

"We're so pleased you've applied to us for a place on the Catering Course, Mr Sullivan," they'll say, smiling kindly. "And how did you get on at school?"

"Brilliant," I'll say. "In fact, so brilliant I found myself ending an undistinguished school career with an indefinite suspension and eight shite grades."

"Oh," they'll say, looking serious, and trying to find my application form from beneath the mess spread across their table. "Then we shall have to reconsider our offer."

So, I thought we might be in a position to help each other out — a bit of career development.

21

Anyway, let me place you in the frame.

It's about this email I got a couple of nights ago. It had this attachment containing half a dozen jpegs.

"Hello," I say to myself, "what's this all about?" and click on the first one.

Well, Mr Hardwick, imagine — imagine my surprise when I see it's a picture of my English teacher — you! — standing really close to the lovely Charmaine Doff in Year Ten. I mean, I know that it's important to provide extra support for students who need help — but Mr Hardwick, I feel that you might have been seriously invading her body space.

So, I click on to the second image, expecting that all will be revealed — at least to my satisfaction, so that I won't have to worry about the moral well-being of a fellow student — and it's worse, Mr Hardwick.

I know that you used to be a happily married man and that things didn't turn out well between you and Mrs Hardwick (or is it Mrs Barraclough?), but I do wonder that you could be so reckless with your reputation.

I can see from the tables and chairs and what-not, that we're looking at an English classroom on the ground floor of the main block, but I don't think that gives you the right to softly stroke the silky hair of an innocent and conscientious schoolgirl, gazing down at her with what I can imagine the newspapers might describe as 'the burning lust of a middle-aged divorcee'.

Flip forward a couple of months and there you are, in the dock at Leicester Crown Court, stammering out some pathetic excuse: "I-I was only h-helping Charmaine with her part as J-Juliet in the school play. Coaching her through her f-first meeting with Romeo."

I can't say that Charmaine feels the same way, Mr Hardwick. I don't know whether she's found the courage to discuss any of this with her mother, but she was pretty 'distraught' when she told me about it — 'ashen-faced and sobbing', in fact.

I won't go through the remaining four pictures, Mr H, they're too intrusive, if you ask me. Shot through the Junior playground window, I would guess, but I do feel we should find a way out of this difficulty.

I admit that I wasn't in school that Thursday you paid a visit to the market. As I said, there's only two of us at home and during these hard times it's sometimes been necessary to help Mum make ends meet. As for the school books that you so sharply spotted, why, I don't know anything about them, but I did wonder whether or not they might have been cleared out by mistake during the annual stock check or something, and maybe a cleaner brought them over? Who knows?

If you could reflect on this matter, I'd be very grateful, Mr Hardwick, and I'll encourage Charmaine to look on your 'rehearsal' with her in a different light, as I'd hate for there to be any unfortunate consequences. I mean, where would a disgraced former teacher find employment in this area?

About the jpegs? I'm sure I can square the photographer. They're not on the Internet yet.

In conclusion, I do think, after all the efforts I'm making on your behalf, that it would be appropriate, for my diligence — is that the right word? — to be recognised by the school. So that when Mrs Nolan withdraws the slip of paper next November, and looks up at the assembled multitude, I think we'll know whose name she's going to read out.

Just a thought, Mr Hardwick.

Waking Early, West Kirby
David Belbin

I have a hangover but that isn't what's stopping me from getting back to sleep. It's remembering. I go back over everything I did last night, recalling pretty much every word said to me, every word I said back, to make sure I didn't make a fool of myself.

Only when I'm certain I did nothing stupid do I look at my watch. Half past five. I've slept less than four hours. Outside, the sun is beginning to bleed across the clear sky. I go downstairs, not caring how much noise I make. Every night, Mum takes two sleeping pills and is dead to the world until at least nine.

I scare my mother. She can't wait for me to go to university (presuming I get the grades). Then she can screw married men, sleep all day and drink a bottle of gin every night without anyone to answer to. I scare my father, too. He's had me to stay once since the divorce. I scare my friends, but at least they tell me why, some of them. I am too articulate, they say. I have this *look* that freezes them out. I take everything too seriously. I always have to be in control.

I scare myself sometimes. *Lighten up*, Mark says to me. A phrase from American TV. *You need to lighten up*. He acts like he cares, but that's probably because he wants to sleep with me. This is something my friends and I used to discuss a lot. How boys only act interested because they want sex. Why did we stop talking about that? Too obvious? No. Everyone states the obvious, all the time. It's because we're all sleeping with our boyfriends now. Except me.

I smell of smoke, sweat and stale perfume. Later, when the water's hot enough, I'll have a bath. In the meantime, I dress and leave the house, walk up Beacon Hill and cross the road into The Common. It's my favourite part of this place, The Common. If you walk far enough, it takes you to the sea. Earlier in the summer, I'd take my books and walk to the part where the trees are at their densest, nearly blocking out the sky. I'd find a hollow to burrow into and I'd read, read until I couldn't absorb any more. Then I'd go to the beach and walk up and down until my head was clear and I was ready to revise again.

The Common is the quietest I've ever known it. Too early for the dog walkers, even. There's a sea breeze and I feel stupid for wearing only a short sleeved T-shirt. I go down the hill and decide to sit for a while, think. I find a familiar hollow and curl up in it. A sharp stone pokes my thigh. I move it. Then I think about sex. I wouldn't mind doing it with someone, just to get it over with. But the only boy I feel safe asking is Mark, and I like him too much. If we had sex, it wouldn't be casual. This is the wrong time to get a serious boyfriend. Mark's going to Cardiff. I'll be in Nottingham. They're too far apart. Thinking about this gives me a dark, heavy feeling at the back of my head. Within minutes, I'm asleep.

I'm woken by heavy footsteps, close by. I check my watch. Quarter to seven. Who walks at this time on a Monday? This isn't a short cut to anywhere. I don't hear a dog. Still, if I have a right to be here this early, so does the walker.

The hollow I'm in is on one of two overgrown slopes, facing each other, with a path running between them. A man is coming down the path very slowly, clumsily. I recognise him. His name is Bob Pritchard. He went out with my mum a few times. I go to the Grammar School with his daughter, Sally.

Bob weaves in and out of the trees. He's drunk, I figure, and hasn't been home yet. He stops to relieve himself and I look away. I realise I'm hungry and thirsty and the water's been on for an hour, so I can have my bath. As soon as Bob leaves, I'll go home. But Bob doesn't seem in a hurry to go. He's leaning on a tree. As I watch, he begins to bang his head against the bark, slowly. I think he might be crying. I watch him do this for a long time then think *Sod it* and get up to go. I'm sure that Bob won't notice me, but he does.

"Hey!" His voice is loud, authoritative. "I want to talk to you!"

Bob, no longer so clumsy, is pushing branches aside, coming up the hill. This ground isn't made for fast escapes. There are big bushes and trees and pitted earth between me and the ridge. Before I can decide what to do, Bob's in front of me.

"How long were you watching me?"

His voice is slightly slurred.

"I haven't been watching. I've been asleep."

"Aah. Out for the night, were you?"

I don't reply.

"You're Kathy's daughter."

Reluctantly, I nod. He smiles lecherously.

"Do you take after your mother?"

"Go away," I mouth, but no words come out.

"I'll bet you were a bad girl last night."

When I reply, I sound like Mum: "Ask your daughter. She was there."

And she was the one being the bad girl, though I don't say this. Bob's still blocking the way down to the path. I decide to brazen it out, walk past him.

As I come towards him, Bob makes a whimpering noise. "She threw me out last night," he explains, almost pleads. "I had to spend the night here."

Close up, Bob reminds me of my father, a seedy, middle-class, middle-aged, middle-management man. He probably got thrown out for fucking around once too often, like my dad did.

"Go home," I say. "She's probably changed her mind."

Bob gives me a sickening smile. "You're a kind girl," he says. "You do take after your mother."

Out of some polite habit, I smile, then try to pass him. That's when he grabs me. A moment later I'm on the ground, pinned down by his heavy body.

"You're a kind girl," he repeats.

I try to kick him but can't move my legs. Bob uses his free hand to grab at my jeans. I cry out. It's more like a yelp than a scream, but there's nobody around to hear me anyhow. That's when Bob punches me in the stomach, hard. Then, while I'm winded, he pulls up my T-shirt, ripping it. He pushes a wad of T-shirt into my mouth and I think — *he's done this before.*

We're in the hollow where I was asleep. What's happening can't be seen from the path below. With one hand, Bob holds me down, while the other tugs at my jeans until they're around my knees. Bob grimaces, realising that he needs both hands to unbuckle his belt. In this fraction of freedom, I reach for the rock I moved earlier, the one that was digging into my thigh.

"You're going to enjoy this," Bob pants and, before he can press down on me again, I smash the rock against his head. Warm blood splashes my cheek and shoulder. His head flops sideways, above mine. Bob doesn't move. I realise he's unconscious. Now I need all my strength to push him off me. I take the torn T-shirt out of my mouth before looking at him. He's on his side, not breathing.

I start shivering and pull up my jeans. The T-shirt is hanging off my chest, exposing my left breast. Bob still isn't moving. The bloody rock is by his head. A half bottle of whisky pokes out of his jacket pocket. I think about all the questions I will have to answer, all the things that people will say. What was I doing on The Common at seven in the morning? How well did I know Bob Pritchard? How long have I been seeing him?

The pool of blood around Bob's head is growing. I do what they taught me in Brownies. I look for his pulse. I think I find one, but it's very faint. There's a phone box fifteen minutes walk away. Ten if I run. But then the questions will start.

This decision will affect the rest of my life. It's not deciding whether to get off with someone you only half like at a party. Whatever I choose to do, I'll go over my motives and my reasoning again and again. And the decision has to be made now. Someone might come along at any minute. Part of my mind is numb, in shock. Another part schemes.

The only thing I've touched is the rock. I pick it up and look around, making sure I've left no traces of myself. Then I hurry down to the path. I walk fast, keeping to the side so I can duck behind a bush if anybody approaches. I pass the tall black beacon that gives my street its name. Now for the difficult bit. My left hand is on my shoulder, holding my T-shirt in place. The right holds the rock, beneath the T-shirt, over my belly. I leave The Common looking like a pregnant urchin.

My luck holds. There's nobody on the street. The milkman's been and gone. I let myself into the house, where I put my T-shirt in with the wash, turn the machine on. I rinse the bloody rock in hot, hot water and open the back door, I hurl the murder weapon into the rockery. Then I run myself a bath. It's not quite as deep as I like, because the washing machine has already used a lot of the hot water. But by the time I get out, all the evidence is gone. I'm clean.

I spend the next four days waiting for someone to say something about Bob Pritchard. The local paper isn't out until Friday, so I start listening to Radio Merseyside news bulletins. Nothing. Maybe they haven't found the body yet. I think about walking across The Common, checking whether Bob's where I left him. But that would be stupid: the killer returning to the scene of the crime. I daren't ring Sally Pritchard, either. We're not good friends. To phone out of the blue would be suspicious.

Thursday is the day of the 'A' levels results. You can turn up at school from midday onwards and get the results in person or have them posted to arrive the next day. Mark rings and I agree to go with him. We wait until one, hoping to avoid the queue, the crowd.

I get the grades I need, Mark doesn't. On our way out, he begins to chatter about what a wonderful time I'm going to have in Nottingham. I want to go to bed with Mark right this minute, I'm so sorry for him. Then I see Sally Pritchard.

She's on the street with a bunch of people who are discussing their results. And she's crying. The guy she was with last Sunday night tries to comfort her but Sally brushes him off. I'm the only one who knows: it isn't her grades she's crying about, it's her dad. For the first and last time, I feel guilty about what I've done. Not for hitting him, I had to do that. But I should have called an ambulance.

Sally's mum gets out of the car and goes over to her. Mrs Pritchard looks heartbroken too. They hug each other. I ought to go over. I ought to say something, though I've no idea what. I hang back, watching Sally and her mum return to their car. Mrs Pritchard gets into the driver's seat. Sally tries to get in the back, finds the door locked. An arm reaches back to open it and I realise there's somebody in the front passenger seat.

Bob Pritchard kisses his daughter, who is careful not to make contact with the big bandage covering the back and side of his head. As she's doing this, Bob looks over his shoulder and sees me. Before our eyes can meet, he turns back.

Then his wife drives away.

Just For a Laugh
Sylvia Hall

"Let Flubber read, Miss. She'll do it, won't you Flub?"

"Don't call her by that name," Miss Penn said.

"It's her name, Miss. She don't mind, do you, Flub?"

I shrugged, picked up a copy of the play and started to read:

"Spread thy close curtain, love-performing night
That runaways' eyes may wink, and Romeo
Leap to these arms untalked of and unseen."

As I read my voice became more expressive; the rhythm held me in its sway. I became beautiful, passionate Juliet pacing her bed chamber.

"Come, night; come, Romeo; come thou day in night;
For thou will lie upon the wings of night
Whiter than new snow on a raven's back."

Shakespeare's words, written so long ago, tripped lightly off my tongue and, amazingly, 10C was held in their spell. Not a murmur — even Will Harris was quiet.

"Well read, Clarissa May," Miss Penn said.

For a moment I basked in glory, then Will Harris leaned back in his chair. "Flub'd make a good Juliet if she weren't so fat, wouldn't she, Miss?"

"That's rather unkind, Will," Miss Penn said.

Will Harris was not to be silenced, not after he'd just handed out a compliment. "I wasn't being nasty, Miss. Flub read it great, made the words sound like they really meant something. But, all them top actresses — they're thin, aren't they?"

Miss Penn ignored him.

"So, Clarissa May," she said, smiling in my direction,

"why do you think Juliet was willing to defy her parents and risk everything to be with Romeo?"

Inside my head I sang out Juliet's frustrations. 'Cos she was trapped, Miss. Trapped inside that ruddy mansion with those awful parents; trapped an' vulnerable an' helpless. She was desperate, Miss. An' believe me, Miss, I know about desperate.

"Well, Clarissa May, I'm waiting. Why was Juliet willing to risk everything?"

"Because..."

My class mates held their breath, waiting to hear what I'd say.

"Because she was gagging for it, Miss."

Instant giggles. We all fell about bubbling with laughter and wasted minutes of the lesson. Brilliant! It was a fine balancing act, keeping my position in the class; you didn't survive long if you were teacher's pet.

When the laughter had died down, Miss Penn gave us her opinion. I listened to her soft voice, the round vowels so different to my own. She started going on about the position of women in Elizabethan times — so we let her get on with it. Ellie was braiding Chelsea's hair; Mo got busy texting and Chantal and Luchia whispered behind their hands. Most of the lads were quiet but only because they fancied Miss and it was a perfect opportunity to ogle her breasts.

"Give me my Romeo and when I shall die
Take him and cut him into little stars."

"That's dead romantic," Stacey Norland said, waving a stick of lip gloss.

Miss Penn nodded, pleased that somebody was listening. When she'd finished reading, she stretched her long legs and stood up. I looked down at my fat thighs encased in shapeless grey school trousers and shrank them into tanned, lean limbs like hers. I gazed at my fingers spread out on the table, plump as sausages, and imagined fine-boned hands. If I looked like Miss, there's no way I'd be a teacher.

What a waste, stupid cow.

At break we hung about the girls toilets gossiping while we passed round a fag. Jenny had a new boyfriend and I wanted to know the low down. Was he a good kisser? I lived vicariously.

"Honest, he's amazing," Jenny crowed. "There we were, snogging like mad — my legs so wobbly I could hardly stand. I'm crying out, 'more, more', and then suddenly, he stops."

"No!" we all gasped.

"Yeah, honest. He holds me away from him and get this, he says, 'Let's take it a bit slower, things that start quickly, end quickly.'"

I nodded. "It's true," I said. "Look what happened to Romeo and Juliet."

Blank stares all round. I don't think they made the connection. Nobody said a word for at least ten seconds, then this girl from my English class came in.

"Miss Penn's looking for you," she said, gesturing to me before she disappeared into a cubicle.

Damn! I'd forgotten about Miss asking me to see her at break. Jenny and I left the cosy comfort of bog life and headed towards the English office. I sailed along in front, shoving through the crowded corridors, parting the waves, while Jenny followed.

"How's it going, Flubber?" a Year Ten lad sang out.

I slammed my hand into his shoulder. "Watch it, Drainpipe," I warned.

Miss Penn wanted to see me about my GCSE course work.

"You are obviously a highly intelligent and sensitive

young woman. So why do you insist on behaving like an idiot and handing in sub-standard work?"

I raised my eyebrows, puffed out my cheeks and made a sort of popping noise as I blew out.

"Are you chewing gum?"

"No, Miss."

"What do your parents think? Don't they want you to make the most of your schooling? If you made the effort you could go to college, even university."

She eyed me closely, hoping I'd crack, spill out my heartfelt frustrations, tell her about the dreadful, insoluble problem that stopped me from studying. I looked at the floor, explored my teeth with my tongue and sighed.

"Don't you want to do well, Clarissa May?"

I stared into her pretty green eyes. "I don't know, Miss."

I could see her trying to find something to say, something that would challenge or inspire me, something that would change my life. She shook her head. I mean, where would you start?

"All right," she said, "off you go."

Jenny was waiting outside. "What she want?" she asked.

"Told me off. Said I was 'disrespectful' in class."

"Bitch."

I took a chunky Kit Kat out of my pocket. "Want some?"

"No, you eat it."

"I shouldn't."

"Don't then."

"I'll just have a nibble."

"Thought you were on a diet."

"I am. I've cut down loads."

36

Jenny laughed. "Don't get too thin. You won't be Flub anymore if you lose weight."

"No, I suppose not," I said.

Walking back down the English corridor, the bell went so we decided to take a short cut through the Drama studio. I opened the heavy door to be confronted by two figures wrapped round each other like cling film. They were so absorbed in a heavy breathing session that they didn't even part when the door wheezed open.

"Did you see who that was?" Jenny demanded, after we'd skirted round them.

"Yep," I replied.

"Nathan Richards," she breathed unnecessarily in an awe-struck voice.

I knew who it was. In Year Seven we'd been in the same class. Nathan Richards, a snub-nosed cheeky little runt, who, to my surprise, had grown up to be the number one stallion of Year Eleven — rated by all the girls as cool and gorgeous — rumoured to have a six-pack and at least one tattoo on his toned and bulging biceps.

"Don't know what he sees in her," Jenny said, peevishly.

I could. His girlfriend was a leggy blonde; no brain but slim hips and breasts like she'd had implants. I knew how the world worked. I ambled off to History, secure in the knowledge that Nathan Richards would never climb my balcony.

I'd always been heavy. Well, how could you expect anything else? My family were built like Sumo wrestlers — Mum, Dad, my brother and me. It's in the genes, Mum said. She was right — mine were size eighteen. I tried a diet once, but they laughed at me and how could I sit there nibbling at a bit of lettuce and tomato while they wolfed down steak and chips? Heart disease, cholesterol, Mum would have none of it.

"Get it down you, Clarissa May. Your Grandma weighed over fifteen stone all her life — and she lived till she was eighty-four."

When the final bell rang, I said good-bye to Jenny. She was staying behind for netball, so I had to cope with the nightmare of the school bus by myself. I hated buses — steps to climb, narrow aisles, small seats. Luckily, I had a long-standing arrangement with the bus driver, Ted, who was pretty hefty himself. Ted understood the needs of the mightily challenged and always let me get on first.

The double-decker was waiting in the bus bay, a pushing crowd round the closed door. I ambled up. There was a bit of moaning and whinging from the little kids as I bulldozed my way through to the front.

"Hey, Flub, leave room for us," a little Year Seven girl, who lived on my street, shouted.

I flicked her pony tail. "Shut up or I'll sit on you."

Appreciative laughter followed as I moved to stand in front of the bus door. It opened and I was about to hoist myself up when I realised it wasn't Ted who was standing, arms outstretched, blocking the entrance. It was a new driver.

He surveyed the restless crowd. "I don't want any pushing and shoving," he shouted. "There's plenty of room for everybody. Is that clear?"

"Where's Ted?" a Year Eleven lad yelled.

"He's sick, so you'll have to put up with me," the new driver snapped. "And I'm not taking any nonsense."

"We want Ted, we want Ted," some kids started to chant.

The new driver looked nervous. "Stay back," he shouted. "You'll get on two at a time, or, or... not at all."

I moved to the front. "I always get on first," I said firmly.

He looked down at me. "Who says so?" he sneered.

"I'm disabled," I answered.

"You're not, Flub, you're just fat," a lad behind me shouted.

I joined in the laughter — I'd had years of practice.

The new driver squared his shoulders. "I'm in charge," he said. "And I'll say who gets on first."

"I have to sit at the front downstairs," I insisted.

His eyes narrowed as he looked down at me. "You're on last," he said. "This bus isn't built to accommodate wide loads."

Everybody burst out laughing. The driver stepped back into his cab and people surged past me; the Upper School kids on top and the little kids hopping on like rabbits, filling all the seats downstairs.

"Sorry, Flub," somebody shouted.

But sorry or not, they all piled onto the bus. Elbows thumped into my arms; I was shoved sideways, my back pack ending up on the ground, my jumper unravelling at the wrist. A heavy trainer crunched my fingers as I scrabbled to retrieve the bag. Finally, when everybody was on board and I'd managed to stand upright, I reached for the pole to hoist myself up. Too late. The doors swished shut. As the bus pulled away, I saw the driver look back — he was laughing.

Tears stung my eyes as I watched the bus disappear round the corner. Now I'd have to endure the humiliation of public transport and pay for the pleasure and I didn't even know if I had enough money. Checking my pockets, I heaped curses upon the callous pig of a driver. Two pound coins and the remains of a Kit Kat. As I stomped off towards the public bus stop, the chocolate provided a snippet of comfort.

There was still a lot of traffic about; parents picking up kids, teachers making a bid for freedom. Miss Penn drove past in a bright red car. Then everything quietened down and there was just me staring out at the playing fields opposite. It started to rain, a fine drizzle. Great, I'd be late home and soaking wet.

I tried to cheer myself up with my favourite dream: my picture in a magazine; I'm four stone lighter and accepting my award as Weight Watchers' Slimmer of the Year. No hope of it coming true. Mum had vetoed Weight Watchers. "It's a rip-off," she said. "Go to Boots, you can get weighed for fifty pence there."

I rummaged in my bag for a snack and found solace in a bag of crisps. I was scooping the last salty bits from the foil, when a presence loomed at my side. The aura was definitely masculine. Tall, lithe, confident, bursting with energy; I could almost smell the testosterone. Hastily shoving the empty crisp packet in my pocket, I glanced sideways to determine what hunk of manhood was standing beside me. None other than Nathan Richards — Number One Stallion.

He swaggered a bit when he saw me looking, but there was no way I was going to show any interest in him. He had enough girls feeding his ego. I hunched my shoulders and looked at the distant hills.

"I'm at the bus stop." His voice was sharp, jagged. "I can't tonight, I'm busy." Pause. "I said, I'm busy, right?"

Out of the corner of my eye I saw him holding his mobile away from his ear while a voice shrilled into empty space. Somebody was giving him a hard time. He nodded his head and rolled his eyes until the voice was silent. Arrogant git. I guessed it was his girlfriend who he was giving the brush off, the same girl he'd been snogging so passionately in the Drama studio.

A few minutes later he was on the phone again, but this time his whole manner had changed. His voice was soft, even tender. "Yeah, I'll be round about seven. 'Course I'm looking forward to it. No, no, I've told her, she's dumped. Yeah, I wanna be with you, too."

The two-timing scally! I scowled at him. He knew I'd been listening and gave me a smug smile. I was standing hating him when I saw Jenny hurrying towards me.

"Thought you were at netball," I said.

"Rained off," she said. "What you doin' here?"

"I missed the bus."

"You left in plenty of time."

"Yeah, well, soddin' bus driver wouldn't let me on. I'm going to report him."

"Never mind," Jenny said, smiling, "we can catch the bus together now."

I could see the delight in her eyes as they took in macho man. It was Nathan Richards she was pleased to see, not me.

She'd still got her eyes on him as she gave me a piece of interesting news. "Hey, did you know Miss Penn's doing *Romeo and Juliet*? There's auditions next week."

I felt a surge of excitement.

"They're looking for a gorgeous, hunky Romeo," she said, aiming the remark pointedly at Nathan. He raised his eyebrows and smiled at her. For a moment, she forgot my presence, coyly gazing at Nathan, smiling sweetly, eyelashes fluttering like bat's wings. I poked her arm; she jumped. "What? Oh, yeah, why don't you go for Juliet, Flub?"

For a brief moment, I entertained the thought. Me as a smouldering, passionate Juliet, delivering my lines with feisty defiance and aching love. Then I heard Nathan's laughter.

41

I turned and glared at him. "What's so funny?" I demanded.

He covered his mouth with his hand. "Nothing."

I fixed him with a deep stare. "You got something to say about me being Juliet?"

"Nah," he giggled.

I stepped closer to him. "Do you remember me?"

He shrugged. "Nah."

"I was in your class in Year Seven," I said.

"Oh, right." His expression clearly read, 'so what?'

"Yeah, I sat in front of you," I said. "But I had to move classes."

"Oh."

"'Cos I was bullied."

"Tough," he said.

"Yeah, it was," I said.

His lip twitched nervously.

"Some horrible little git who sat behind me kept calling me names," I said, shooting him a full-beam glare of hate.

He turned his head away, muttering something under his breath.

I leaned close to him, so close I could smell his hair gel. He tensed up, his eyes half closed.

I smiled. "Don't worry," I said. "It's made me a much stronger person."

His eyes opened wide; he looked relieved. "Really?"

"Yeah," I said. "I've developed a super-thick skin. Insults, name-calling, injections at the hospital — I show no pain. And, thanks to people like you, I've developed a great sense of humour. Training to be a comedian, me."

He nodded. "Oh, good. That's all right, then."

"Yeah," I said. "You could say it was the making of me."

His phone buzzed. I reached out and took it from him. The message on the screen was succinct and presumably from girlfriend number one — it read, "U SHIT".

"My word, we're everybody's favourite person, aren't we?" I tutted. "Dear, oh dear, let's get rid of it, shall we?" I erased the message and handed back the phone. Nathan looked bewildered.

"Introduce me, then," Jenny chirped brightly, coming over and standing next to us.

Instantly, Nathan relaxed. He was back on familiar territory — this type of encounter, he could handle. He pulled himself up to his full height and smiled down at Jenny. "What's your name, gorgeous?" he asked, cocking his head to one side and giving her a look.

"Jenny," she cooed.

"Nice name," he said.

"Yes, isn't it?" I said, shaking Jenny's hand from my arm. "And mine's Clarissa May."

His mouth twitched into a rather annoying smile. "No, it's not," he said, "it's Flubber."

"So, you do remember me?"

"Yeah, sort of," he said.

I don't know if it was the threatening look on my face or the fact that I was only a few centimetres from his nose, staring directly into his eyes, but he began to look uncomfortable.

"It was just a joke," he said.

"What?"

"Calling you Flubber."

"Really?"

"Yeah, I didn't mean anything by it."

I nodded slowly, my eyes still glaring into his. "No, 'course not," I said.

The throb of a bus engine broke the tension between

43

us. Nathan darted to one side and was almost round me, heading for the oncoming bus, when I caught hold of his blazer and pulled him back.

"Wait a minute," I said. "I was first in the queue."

He gave me a hard look. "Shove off, Flubber."

I clenched my fist, took a deep breath, gritted my teeth and let fly. I hit him smack on his neat up-tilted nose. Everything went into slow motion. His pupils dilated, his mouth opened into a wide 'O' and blood bloomed from both nostrils.

Jenny twittered and spluttered at my side. "Flub! What did you do that for?" she shrieked.

I stepped back and wiped my fist on Nathan's blazer. "What do you expect from a girl called Flubber?" I said.

Nathan was whimpering. "I-I didn't mean it. I didn't know the name would stick," he gurgled through hands clamped round his nose. "It was just for a laugh."

Jenny put a comforting arm round his shoulders. "You've hurt him. Why did you do it, Flub?"

I shrugged and began to walk towards the bus.

"Sorry," I said. "It was just for a laugh."

Karma Drama (extract)
B.K. Mahal

I read the questionnaire, checked it was for me —
Sushminder, yes it was, and, as expected of me,
answered truthfully:

"Could you walk into an evening soiree unescorted?"

I didn't know there was a choice.

"What is a hors' d'oeuvres?"

Do the words 'red light district' give the game away?

"Do you know how to fold a napkin in five different
ways?"

I'll have you know I'm very competent in origami. I
can do a plane, a dog, swan, tower and Merry Hill
Shopping Centre. Dad taught me. He was a proper chef,
and he doesn't put that pongy masala in everything like
you do here.

"Are you confident and capable enough to eat canapé
without spoiling your lipstick?"

What kind of question is that?

"Do you know how to get up gracefully from the
floor?"

Not applicable.

"Do you know how to welcome a foreign dignitary?"

Sat-sri-akal, aslam alekum or *namaste*. If any of
these fail, my dad says playing bhangra lightens up
anyone with a sack of potatoes for a face.

"Can you dance elegantly in a club?"

Have you been to one lately?

"Name three ways of initiating a conversation."

Get stuffed.

Get stuffed.

Leave me alone.

"Do you know how to take a compliment?"

Are you giving me one? If so, then yes; if not, why so?

"What does your daily diet consist of?"

At the moment it's three praatha's or some cornflakes from Dave in the kitchen. Then I snack on what you lot call double roti and what our lot call bread till mid-day. Usually I'll make do with pasta or pizza later — anything without chillies. Dad and I then get whatever meal's on at Quality in the evening. Today it's Muglai. Can't wait.

"Do you know how to be sincere?"

I'll have you know I am demonstrating the very qualities right now.

Having finished quicker than the others I checked the time; it was still 12.28 and I was still stuck in Delhi with a hopeful mother in Dudley awaiting my re-birth as a proper person, no, I mean a proper girl. Around me, stupefied eyes and fidgets pondered over the questions. Sanjana was still writing furiously, while Daz Sidhu, stuck on the first question, touched the tip of her nose with her camel-like tongue. After a few more paragraphs had been scribbled, Miss Laila dashed back into the hotel's conference room. Her thick black hair was now in a tidier bun and her pale burgundy lipstick shone deeply from another re-application. As if worried by our looks of concern, she assured us that the results would be collected by her PA and that we would receive these tomorrow, whereupon our individual programs of study, to turn us into real ladies, would be administered.

"Each of you will have deficits in a few different areas. Some of you may have them in all."

That last bit was directed at me. You could just sense it. Miss Laila then went on to explain how a small piece of paper called a certificate would enable us to access parts of society that were hitherto closed. I asked if it could be purchased at a rock-bottom but worthy price. She said, "No. Not on your nelly."

I told her I didn't have a nelly and even if I did she wouldn't get to it. She asked if I would ever like to see Dudley again, to which I replied, "Yes."

"Shut up then." So I did.

For the remainder of the lesson, everyone except me had to introduce themselves to the rest of the gaggle. Miss Laila reckoned they knew far too much about me anyway. These harrowing introductions prompted another search for a Murray Mint. Quickly, I found one of the remaining two and, when nobody was watching, threw it into my mouth which was clammed together by the dryness brought about by the air conditioning. The Murray Mint clung to the inside of my cheek.

"Well, what can we conclude from that?" asked Miss Laila, after the introductions.

The only thing I could conclude was that among us there was a Sanjana, Daz, Abha, Amrit, Zafreen, Gurmeet, Saroj, Ria and Faz for Fazana. Abha was a particularly lovely daft name, and I earmarked potential friendship with her. Three of them were over twenty-five, two of which classed themselves as home-makers. Amrit was an IT consultant heading for America, but needed that all-important advice on how to pass the etiquette test at her workplace, to guarantee her a place on the employment programme. She couldn't bear the idea of being labelled a freshie. The rest had despairing parents who had long since tired of one's unladylike behaviour. A real bunch of desperadoes, we were.

When Miss Laila spoilt the fun and subjected us to a powerpoint presentation. I found myself doing that thing with my eyes when they don't listen to my brain. I didn't really want to watch, but I did. The presentation informed its pupils that assessment would be conducted through covert observations.

"That's against our human rights," I told Miss Laila.

"We're in India. Has one heard of our record lately?"

"It ain't nothing to be proud of," I replied, thoroughly disgusted and sounding like Mum.

But before I could declare that a revolution should have its roots in our class, I was hailed to settle down to watch the rest of the silly presentation on how to make a good impression in fifteen seconds. My eyes, as usual, did not listen to my brain and I sat gormlessly. From what I could gather, to make a good impression, it takes a well-pressed outfit and plastered eye shadow. One mustn't shake one's hands, but instead make demure eye contact. One should introduce one's self as 'Mus' instead of Miss. One should stand with the string in one's back pulled taut. Before disclosing much about one's self, one should listen to those that are in greater esteem in that thing called a social circle again. One should always ponce about gracefully and nibble food grasped from a silver tray. One should never eat more than one thing from these trays. One must appreciate one's self before one appreciates another. One should achieve this all within fifteen seconds, and finally, one should refer to humans as one, even when we are six billion and counting.

Miss Laila beamed with the thought of having impressed Sanjana, the hotelier's daughter. She, taking it more seriously than the average among us, was already miming some of the rules to herself. Her brows all tweaked and her arms all floaty, fancy-like, as she shook hands with an imaginary friend. Miss Laila was impressed.

Abrupt instructions for us to pair up with a person of our choosing were dished out. We were now expected to role-play the perfect first encounter. Slightly alarmed, like a scaredy-cat, I sat still in my chair and chose to be a passive participant.

"Acting isn't my forté," I told Miss Laila, "I was born just too honest for my own good."

Miss Laila did not hear me, though, as she instructed Sanjana on how to spread her smile more evenly on her face. Another four pairs formed quickly, which left a quite eager-to-perform but annoyed Faz begrudging my existence.

Sanjana and Daz role-played first and began pecking each other lightly on the cheek, like the French.

"Why don't they just marry each other?" whispered Faz.

This made me giggle uncontrollably — a near-impossible feat to accomplish since my arrival in Delhi. But it was from this point on I began to co-operate.

Sanjana and Daz pulled off a fine performance, followed by some ordinary ones. Perfectly bland introductions, speaking in complete sentences and mimicking one another's disposition, lit up Laila's face. She wasn't content for too long, though, and began to comment on their slapdash approach to standing. Some of them wobbled, you see. Faz said she didn't want to practice, for she came from a place called the method school of acting. I said of course she did, not knowing what she meant exactly, and certainly incapable of asking, as that would mean I didn't know in the first place. Anyway, I didn't have time, as we became further consumed by laughing at the others' more serious take on life. We stayed put, and, like two theatre critics, evaluated those performances that might have killed a lesser man's senses.

Faz then asked Miss Laila bluntly when we would get to the fun part.

"Resisting is a sign of good breeding."

"Only if you're a dog," I quipped. Nobody laughed except Faz, who gave a resounding cackle as back-up. Official friends we were now, you see. Ignoring me, Miss Laila jumped onto the second part of the programme, and held up a framed certificate. Her own devised royal crest was stamped at the bottom. Ever so overcome with emotion was she that Laila floated about the room awhile and caressed the frame.

"You'd like one, wouldn't you?"

Zafreen nodded, eagerly. "I reckon I could forge that easy. It ain't nothing but a bit of parchment paper and calligraphy."

"I'd like to see you try," dared Miss Laila, who went on to lecture us about the absurdity of attempting to do such a thing. Apparently each one of those certificates was numberised and linked to the Asian continent's database. And there was me, worried about nuclear missiles.

"Anyone who has an inkling you're a fake, and that's it, kaput, schmut, *facut*. The database won't lie for anyone."

I asked Miss Laila why anyone would think I was fake.

"Well, you are a bit of a nothing, are you not?"

"Not! Anyway, why must I be a something?"

"Because you can."

"I can jump off the Qutub Minar too, but I won't."

"One can be anything they want to be in life."

I wondered whether this might be true, because if it was then I could be an elephant or a butterfly. But since we could only be some things in life and since I couldn't be an elephant, that Laila had just told a right fat porky.

"Here in India, we believe in the spirit of meritocracy. Believe in yourself, your people, your country, and all good things will come to you — wealth and status," said Ria with her mushroom haircut, hoping to unperplex my quite befuddled-looking smile.

I mentioned that what she had said was a lot like the American Dream?

"No, a lot like the Indian Dream," she replied, all defensive and perking up behind her trench.

Independence Day wasn't until August 15th, so I wondered where this bout of patriotism sprung from.

"Only those that truly belong to a nation are patriotic." Daz sprayed her wrist with some Kenzo and licked it, only to do it again. It was gin, Faz informed me.

"I belong," I told them, all put out.

"One that has to say they belong, does not."

"Go on then, say your national anthem."

"Wha...?"

They demanded again that I sing the British national anthem.

"C'mon, how does it go, Sushminder?"

I stayed shtum.

"Surely you *know*, what with you being all patriotic an' all," barked Gurmeet.

"You've misinterpreted for your own dastardly point of view. I didn't say I was patriotic."

Before I could tell them all (including Miss Laila who didn't happen to intervene in a situation some would call 'picking on a person') that I was perfectly fine in my own mess of ignorance, I was already fumbling through the maze in my mind to allay my concern. Maybe they were right about me not knowing where I belonged. If a countryman can't make an effort to learn the anthem then perhaps they just weren't committed enough.

Cagney and Lacey was the only tune that came to mind, so I tried: "Der der. Der der. Der der der der der. Der der der der d-d-der."

Unconvinced, they sneered.

"T. J. Hooker, perhaps?"

"Pa."

It was enough that Daz, Sanjana and Gurmeet huffed at me, but when they rolled their eyes at me, well that got me in a twist.

"Don't you dare smirk back at me, you smirkers," I told them, ready to run away and attack all at once. "So what if I don't know that doldrums of an anthem. Which decent person does? Only sports stars, the Prime Minister and the Queen bother. That must mean something, hey. Anyway, nationalism is evil. You have to believe their lies, play their roles. All for what — so you feel you belong. Ha, I laugh in the face of a crap song."

"Oh, you Brindians — Sushi-minder, you're..."

"Ya, you're all the same," whined Gurmeet, finishing off Ria's sentence.

I wondered what she meant by that. After all, I was sent to this forsaken place because I was so alien and now this lot here were telling me I'm normal for my kind. Gurmeet, all haughty, tucked a silk of hair behind her studded ears. From underneath her fringe, hollow blue contact lenses jeered at me. Around her stood the rest of her merry men with their dramatic facial expressions and Mutley smiles. Each of them trying hard to evoke a frenzied response from my calm exterior, but not on this day. No. I was going to be Miss Cool, strolling on a Goan sea-front with waves calling for me. Just watch me. Nothing was going to get at me.

When I could not pretend to look unaffected by their 'look-at-me-I-know-my-anthem' expressions, my head sank into my shoulders. I was sick of 'em. These that were so damn concrete. All their words had meaning. Even their gestures spoke. Well, boo-bloody-hoo, I scolded myself. Why, all of a sudden, out of the grey could I not stand people who knew what they were? I'd flamin' well grown up with them. Kully — the sister that was the embodiment of perfection with her gob and appearance intact; even Budgie, the brother who knew that the holy grail of a Mercedes would be the making of him. Kiz was turning out all concrete, too. She'd gone and left me behind with her ideas on a career in aviation.

Relief bit my analysis when I found the last of those Murray Mints. I tore open the wrapper and threw it, like a fish to a seal, into the back of my throat. Bad idea. Lodged somewhere between my tonsils and throat, I choked myself from a brown to a purple. Urging those around me to come to my aid, I flapped my arms as if to take off. They, though, had other important things to do, such as sit-chit. Squirming and jerking on my seat, I coughed feebly to encourage the mint to see the clear light.

"You feeling fit, Sush?"

I shook my head and pointed towards my tonsils to show Faz that I was on the verge of dying by Murray Mint. Death — make it decent, Dad once said. To die by confectionery was anything but. After some bumbling, Faz rose and with one swift swing whacked her big leather satchel onto my back. Out popped the Murray Mint, only to slide across the table of polished veneer.

Miss Laila let out a scream. "Oh. Oh. I thought it was a rat."

"See, she can't even eat properly," said a voice that could have belonged to anybody.

Unable to speak and unable to walk, I tried hard to do both. After a few more moments of gathering my senses, I let these Laila lasses know that anyone could choke at any time, this time it just happened to be me; and secondly, even if I couldn't eat, I had plenty of other skills in my repertoire. Drawing, high-jumping and turning civil moments into laughable ones, are all something they could come and learn from me. So there!

Kiss Kiss
Gwen Grant

24th December 1956

So, here I am, sixteen years old and fed up to the back teeth. There was no good fairy at my christening. Probably fell down a hole because there are plenty of holes round here to fall into.

This town in full of holes.

Pits all round us and miners and pit lads who come in here looking like pandas with their eyes ringed with coal dust.

"Ounce 'a baccy, duck," they go, staring at me with bloodshot eyes circled with black.

They get washed at the pit baths and forget they've got eyes.

This is one of the best winters I remember because when I look out of the shop window, I can see the whole street glittering and snow plastered to the sides of the lamp-posts so that they look like maypoles, only needing a handful of ribbons to finish them off.

Mr Grogan came back from delivering the Orders, looks at me, then says, "You going out tonight, then?"

"Of course I'm going out. It's Christmas Eve. I'm going to the Palais."

"Tut, tut," he goes. "Never in, you're not. No wonder you were late this morning."

But I wasn't late this morning, because I got up with our Joe and walked him to work. He starts at half past seven. It was bitter cold when we got outside, but I was sick of lying in bed, watching the clock tick tock tick tock tick tock all night.

I was glad I'd put my stilettos in my bag because it had started to snow. It was so heavy, it was already lying and there was a bit of a wind, so before we'd got to the end of the street we looked like snowmen.

That was when Joe said, "I'm signing on for the Army. I'm not waiting to be called up. I'm fed up of the life here. There's got to be more to it than this."

I always knew he'd go.

"When are you going to sign on?" I asked, and he said probably the first week in the New Year.

"Then I'll be gone by Spring."

That makes me sick. I want to get away from this town, too, but where my Mam'll say, "Good idea," to our Joe, "get yourself off and learn a trade," to me she goes, "You are not going to Canada, full stop."

The Canadians have taken over a little shop in the town and plastered the windows with posters of Canadian mountains, Canadian lakes, Canadian cities and Canadian sunsets.

I took one look at them and fell in love.

EMIGRATE TO CANADA, they say. A NEW COUNTRY. A NEW LIFE.

I need a new life.

The thing is, you can go to Canada at sixteen if your mam and dad'll sign to let you go. They pay your fare, give you a chaperone, a room of your own and a job in Calgary.

And I want to go. I want to see Calgary. I want to live there. I want a chaperone. And I want a job and a room of my own but I can't have anything unless my Mam and Dad sign, and my Mam won't.

I said to Joe, "You're lucky you can escape," and he goes, "Well, I don't want to be stuck at the factory all my life and I don't want to go down the pit, so it's the Army or nothing."

And that's the end of that conversation.

Mr Grogan says again, "What time did you get here, then?" and I turn away because I know what he wants me to say.

He wants me to say I got here early.

But I won't.

"I got here on time," I tell him, but I think he knows I'm lying, because when I left our Joe, I caught a bus into town and got to the shop too early.

When I put my key in the lock, I was surprised because it opened straight away and I didn't have to use my big key in the other lock.

I stepped inside. The shop has a kind of velvety darkness and it's warm and smells of rich tobacco. I love this first minute of the day, when everything is quiet and fresh.

I took a deep breath, then nearly choked because I heard a noise, a soft, odd sound.

My first thought was that someone had broken in. We have piles of boxes in the cellar, all with dozens of cartons of cigarettes in them, then there's all the packets of tobacco.

Steal that lot and you'd make a fortune.

But then I realised the sound wasn't coming from the cellar. It was coming from upstairs. From the office. So maybe somebody was after the money in the safe.

That's when I went upstairs.

I took my shoes off and kept to the sides of each step because this whole building is about four hundred years old and the stairs creak.

Pad, pad, pad, I went and when I was halfway up, my head level with the bottom of the open office door, I peered in and there was Mr Grogan and that blonde woman from the Bank and whatever they were doing half undressed, they were not stealing any money.

If Mrs Grogan had been there, she'd have killed them, so I headed back down those stairs as fast as I could before they saw me.

I opened the back door again and went out, shutting it behind me so carefully it only made the tiniest little click. I walked down the yard and stood under the archway for ages until I thought it was safe, then went back up singing.

Miss Simmons, who owns the shop and whose house is on the opposite side of the courtyard, suddenly looks out of her kitchen window and taps on the glass.

"Good morning, dear," she cries, and I shout, "Morning, Miss Simmons," so loudly, I saw her flinch.

I went back to the door and put my key in the lock again but this time when I turned it, the door wouldn't open and I had to use the big key in the bottom lock before I could get in.

So, I thought, Mr Grogan had been down and locked the door! Too late, Mr Grogan!

There was no sound in the shop and because of all my messing about, I was now ten minutes late. The clock on the back wall showed it had just gone half past eight and the shop should have been open.

Where was Mr Grogan?

I took off my coat, hung it up and went into the shop. That was when I saw the bag with my stilettos in it sitting on top of the counter. I'd forgotten to take it with me when I went back out.

My blood went cold, so cold I could feel it trickling through my veins.

When he'd come downstairs, had Mr Grogan seen my bag?

Did he know I'd already been in the shop once?

Scariest of all, did he know I'd seen him and the blonde?

I picked my bag up, just as a voice behind me said,

"Late again, Lamour," but I was ready for him, because I'd smelt him. He always smelt of a sharp spicy aftershave.

But I hadn't heard Mr Grogan come down the stairs, which meant he had come down in the same way I went up, keeping close to the sides, making sure they didn't creak, and why would he do that?

Then I wondered where the blonde from the Bank was. Had she left?

If she'd tried to go out the back way, me and Miss Simmons would have seen her and she wouldn't have risked that, not with her and Mr Grogan both being married.

And the shop door at the front was still bolted.

"I said, 'Late again', Lamour," Mr Grogan repeated nastily, and I said, "Sorry, Mr Grogan. It was the snow."

I didn't look at him because I knew what I would see. I would see a big red face, black eyebrows and straight black hair. And I'd see teeth like tombstones, so big and white, I always duck when he smiles in case he bites a chunk out of me.

I make myself look at him in the end but he's not looking at me.

He's looking at my bag.

"That yours?" he asks.

"No," I say, then pick up the bag and drop it just where he can't reach it, on top of the box of Players cigarettes which I'd left in the shop last night, ready for filling out Orders this morning.

Mr Grogan takes all the Orders out.

"Six hundred Players cigs. Four hundred Capstan Full Strength cigs. A thousand Park Drive cigs. Same Woodbine cigs. Three packets tobacco. Two pipes. Three Dunhill lighters. Two packets of Passing Cloud cigs. Twelve cartons of matches."

And so on and so on and so on.

When the Orders are filled, Mr Grogan piles them into his van and he's gone until they're all delivered.

Where was the blonde?

She was like a little satin pin-cushion, all plumped up and pink and white.

I could imagine Mr Grogan pinching her and not leaving a mark on her little plump body.

She comes into the shop all the time.

"Mr Grogan in?" she whispers, sweetly sweetly. "I've a query on your account."

I sigh and shout, "Mr Grogan, you're wanted," and up he comes from the cellar, smiling that great white smile.

He lifts the flap of the counter and steps back but not very far, so she has to push past him.

They think I don't see all this, you know.

Then, grinning, he slams the flap shut and they go upstairs to the office where he shuts the door with a snap.

He's worried I came in early and saw them but I'm not going to let him know I did.

If he found out, I'd be the one worried.

I don't trust Mr Grogan. He always looks at me as if he's hungry.

He's still standing behind me.

"So, what time did you say you got here?" he asks again, the smell of his aftershave really strong.

"Five minutes ago," I say, but looking at the clock, I see it's almost half an hour since I first arrived.

He nods, then kicks at the box of cigarettes with his foot, staring at my bag.

I can almost feel his hands itching to get hold of it.

"You'd best go and get them shutters down," he says

finally. "By the time this shop's open, we'll have lost a day's takings."

Opening the big drawer under the counter, I take out the key. A noise behind us makes him turn. He's worried about it and goes into the back room. Whilst he's gone, I pick up the bag, take out my shoes and slip them on, then shove the bag into one of the cupboards.

Then, I lift the counter flap and open the shop door.

Outside, I have to unlock the padlock on the iron bar which goes across the shutters, take the bar out, take down the first shutter and haul it through the shop and into the back.

Then I do the same with the second shutter.

They weigh a ton so I was struggling and not thinking about the blonde.

Until I saw her standing in the shop, in front of the counter.

I nearly jumped out of my skin.

"Where did you come from?" I say.

She smiles.

"I came through the door. Didn't you see me?"

I shook my head because to see her, I would have had to have X-ray vision because she didn't come down the street from the Bank.

She had been the noise in the back and where she had come from was the office upstairs. When I looked at her more closely, I could see her little plump pink and white face was pinker than ever.

Mr Grogan's bristles had done that.

After I'd dumped the shutter, I went back to the shop door and looked up the street towards the Bank. The morning was dark so from the Bank windows, great golden squares of light fell onto the snow. The blonde came and stood beside me and that was how we both saw that the snow between the shop and the Bank hadn't a single footprint on it.

She turned slowly round to stare at me, her eyes like little chips of ice, her mouth hard.

So, I said to myself, that's what you get for being clever, Lamour, because now she knows that you know she was upstairs with Mr Grogan.

I shivered, wondering if she would tell him.

"Do you want Mr Grogan?" I asked.

She nodded.

"Is it about our account?"

She nodded again.

Suddenly, I got mad.

"Miss Simmons is in. Shall I fetch her instead?" I offered, and Mr Grogan appeared behind me like a genie out of a lamp, so close, he could have breathed for me if he'd wanted.

"I'll see to this," he snapped, then he looked down at my feet and then at the top of the Players box, but all he said was, "You get on."

And that was that.

Miss Simmons came in, the day started and I was busy the whole time but I was really glad to see Mr Grogan go out with the deliveries.

I can't wait for tonight. It'll be great at the Palais. You get all the pit lads from Hitwell and Waterwell as well as from the town pits. They pour into that dance hall, flush with money and wild to dance.

"You dancin'?" they ask.

"You askin'?" you say, then you laugh and you're on that floor in double quick time.

If the music's fast enough, you can get a bop in so long as you're in a corner and Mr Reilly doesn't see you.

You're not supposed to do bebop or jive at the Palais and if Mr Reilly catches you, he orders you off the floor.

He goes round again when the band plays slow

because smooching isn't allowed either, tapping you on the shoulder if you get too close and still with each other.

"Split!" he yelps. "One more warning and you're banned."

But all you want to do is smooch because there's something fabulous about being so close to a lad, you can almost walk through each other, and there's a band playing and you can hear him breathing and feel his breath on your neck or in your hair and there's this faint small of tobacco and Brylcreem and soap and he murmurs with a voice gone all husky and his huge hands are on your back and even through your blouse, you can feel them inching hotly up and down your skin.

I can never decide if smooching is better than bopping, when you're whirling and jiving, darting in and out to the beat, obeying the orders of the lad's hands and his eyes and his laugh, swinging round and round until you're dizzy and you don't care, then skimming through their legs and, if he's a really good dancer, he'll throw you over his head and you'll land, still dancing, spinning, spinning, spinning until you're hot and sweating and your heart's beating like crazy and you are crazy and that's the best feeling in the world, as well.

No wonder I'm dying for tonight.

The only problem is that when the pit lads are all together, they fight like there's no tomorrow.

Upstairs in the Palais, there's a big room with chairs and tables and a long counter where they serve coffee and sandwiches but they don't serve booze. They don't have to because most of the pit lads are half-cut when they come in.

That's where the trouble starts.

Last week, you couldn't get up the stairs because the

pit lads were fighting. By the time the bouncers had got it sorted out, it was almost the end of the night, then it all stopped, anyway, because the lads want the last waltz.

Chuck came into the shop earlier.

I like Chuck. He's a pit lad and he's tough and nice and good-looking.

So good-looking, he makes my heart miss a beat.

"Twenty Capstan Full Strength, sexy," Chuck grins, and before I can blink, Mr Grogan comes out of the back when I didn't even know he was in.

"Sexy!" he goes. "Who you calling sexy? This is a decent shop. You watch your tongue and you," he turns to me, pointing with a big nicotine-stained finger, "you stop encouraging him."

Chuck's nice face goes hard, then he leans over the counter.

"Who you talking to?" he says. "Why don't you just sod off?"

Mr Grogan hesitates, staring at Chuck. He didn't expect this. But Chuck is big and his eyes are blue and fierce, so all Mr Grogan does is point at me again and snap, "I shall want a word with you, Madam. I shall have to report this to Miss Simmons."

Then he goes.

I sigh.

"Chuck," I say, "you've probably lost me my job and I can't afford to be out of work."

As it is, I have to do two nights every week at the Mental Health café, waitressing, just to make ends meet. Otherwise, I'd be going around stark naked because without that extra money, I couldn't afford to buy a handkerchief, let alone a coat or a skirt or a blouse.

But Chuck just says, "He won't sack you. You going to the Palais tonight?"

I nod.

"See you there, then," he grins, and just for a second, I hesitate, because if you see a lad there, you miss all the new lads that might come in, so I just said, "Okay."

I love kissing.

Especially kissing mouths I haven't kissed before.

Although Chuck's a good kisser.

The second the clock struck six, I was clearing up in the shop, putting up the shutters, slamming the iron bar across them, slapping on the padlock, locking it, then throwing the key back into the drawer.

I like the shop when the shutters are up and there's only the one light lit. It gleams on the different coloured fag packets and packets of tobacco and tins of snuff and piles of matches and boxes with beautiful silver lighters inside them.

There's Players in their blue and white packets, Passing Clouds and Capstan, Gold Flake with its gold packet, Woodbines, Park Drives and all the others in their bright jackets, and then there's the shiny black of the pipes all set out on the shelves inside the glass cases, sitting on their little bits of blue velvet, some of them glowing dark red, and there's crystal ash trays and everything you need to smoke and it's all shining together and smelling sweet as honey.

Sometimes I wished I smoked but it makes me sick.

I dragged my coat on, slipped off my stilettos, fished out my bag from the back of the cupboard, dropped them in, put the bag in my big bag, changed into my flat shoes then stepped into the yard.

It was pitch black outside with only a chink of light coming from Miss Simmons's kitchen window.

The yard had been swept but even through the fresh snow laying on the cobbles, it still shone ice.

I was glad I'd got out of the shop without seeing Mr

Grogan again but as I stepped onto the snow, walking carefully down the middle of the yard, trying not to slip, behind me I heard a crunching sound and when I turned, I saw the delivery van slicking over the snow towards me.

And I knew it was going to run me down.

The van wasn't making a sound. That's what I couldn't understand. It was coming towards me like a ghost van.

I stood there, unable to move, until I heard Miss Simmons scream.

"Lamour! Get out of the way."

Then I seemed to wake up and leapt for safety, smashing head first into the wall as the van slid past, so close, I felt a rush of air as it went. It didn't stop moving until it crashed into the double doors at the end of the archway which closed the yard off from the street.

Miss Simmons ran across to me.

I was stunned for a second, then something warm trickled down my forehead and when I put my hand up, it came away red with blood.

I started shaking and Miss Simmons put an arm round me.

"Come into the house, Lamour. For heaven's sake, what happened?"

Then Mr Grogan was rushing down the yard, shouting, "Didn't you hear me, Lamour? I tried to warn you. The van slid away and I couldn't stop it."

It sounded as if he was acting in a Play.

Miss Simmons wiped the blood away and made me a cup of tea but I drank it standing up.

I didn't want to talk to Mr Grogan. I just wanted to go straight home.

I had some homework to do. Shorthand. That's what had kept me awake all night. For homework, you're supposed to take down the News in shorthand every night and last night, I couldn't remember the short form for 'Chancellor of the Exchequer' and from one hour to the next, I was trying to think what it was.

Chancellor of the Exchequer.

Chancellor of the Exchequer.

Now, I suddenly remembered how you wrote it. It goes like this: ⨍

Why would I remember that when I'd almost been killed by a runaway van?

There's no evening class for another two weeks, anyway, so it could have waited, but no, it had to come when I was almost dead with fright.

By the time I'd drunk the tea, Mr Grogan had driven the van back up the yard to the garage.

The funny thing was that behind those double doors was his wife, Mrs Grogan, who had been only an inch away from opening them.

"My fingers," she said shakily, "were already on the latch, Lamour. I actually had it in my hand and I was just going to turn it and step inside." She shivered. "If I had done that, it would have been the last thing I ever would have done."

Mr Grogan was back by then but he said nothing, just looked from Mrs Grogan to me and back from me to Mrs Grogan, baring his teeth at me in what was supposed to be a smile.

I put my cup down on the sink and said, "I'm off, then, Miss Simmons. See you tomorrow," and got out of that house.

Outside, I looked into the shadowy darkness of the yard but there was nothing to see.

No van sliding down to kill me, anyway.

I went through the double doors, edging through one

I only half opened, out into a different world.

It was brilliant on the street. All white and beautiful as if the whole mucky town had changed and I wasn't living in a place full of pits, at all, but in some shining dream world.

Across the road, Chuck was standing in a shop doorway and he walked over as I stepped into the street.

"Thought I'd wait and see you to the bus," he said, taking my arm. "He didn't bother you again, did he?" he asked, jerking his head towards the shop.

"No," I said. "He didn't."

I didn't tell Chuck about the van but he brought it up himself.

"What was that crash? I thought those doors were going to fall out."

"It was the van," I told him. "The brakes weren't on and it slid down the yard."

Chuck left me at the bus stop.

There was a queue a mile long but when I was finally on, I waved to him through the window and he shouted, "See you tonight," which didn't please me, really.

I didn't want to get into any going steady.

I paid my fare and turned back to the window, just in time for the lights to change and the bus to stop outside the Canada shop.

There was someone still inside because there was a light on. I decided that in the morning I would go down and ask if they had any spare posters. I could put them up on my pitiful half-inch of bedroom wall and pretend I was really in Canada, actually looking out at them.

I share a bedroom with my sisters. Two of them. That's all I need say about that.

Somebody sat next to me and a voice said, "It's me, Lamour," and in the bus window, I saw the reflection of a woman.

Mrs Grogan.

I turned round and said, "I didn't know you caught this bus, Mrs Grogan," and she shook her head, "I don't usually." Then she went on, "I only want you to tell me one thing. Is he seeing her?"

I stood up.

"Excuse me," I muttered. "I've just seen my sister."

Actually, I'd seen our Rose before but I hadn't wanted to acknowledge her.

Now, I pushed past Mrs Grogan.

Rose frowned when I sat down.

"What's the matter with you?" she said. "Have you forgotten we're related? And what've you done to your head? It's bleeding."

The last I saw of Mrs Grogan, she was staring at me through the bus window as me and our Rose got off.

But I didn't care.

I didn't want to talk to her about the blonde in the Bank.

When I got in, my Mam was so mad about my head and about the van that she was all for putting on her coat and going to see Miss Simmons.

"What can they be thinking of?" she cried.

But I persuaded her not to.

After tea, I took the news down in shorthand and got the short form for 'Chancellor of the Exchequer' in, then I went and got ready for the Palais.

Joe was going, too, so we took the bus back into town together.

It was good at the Palais but something was wrong. I couldn't seem to get happy. I was hot and my neck ached. I trailed upstairs and had a cup of coffee, sitting all on my own at one of the tables, until I got sick of that and went back down.

The pit lads hadn't arrived so it was quiet on the dance floor.

I looked for Chuck but couldn't see him anywhere.

I danced all night but still I didn't see him. I had to leave before the dance ended to catch the last bus because my Dad waits for me at the bus stop. But there was a queue for the cloakroom and by the time I had my coat, I knew I'd have to run for it.

On the way out, I bumped into our Joe.

"Make sure you're on that last bus," he grinned, as him and this girl went off down the street.

I ran as fast as I could but I got to the corner just as the bus was pulling away.

My head was splitting.

I thought I would try and catch the bus at the next stop so I ran down the road, past the old school, then on under the trees which shivered in the wind, puthering snow down my neck.

I could have cut across the park but I wasn't that stupid so I went around, the park heavy with snow and shadow at my side.

Then it was up past the old church and round the corner just in time to see the bus sweep by without stopping because there was nobody at the bus stop, was there?

I ran on, trying to keep the bus lights in sight.

Once, I slipped, falling full length, all my breath knocked out, but before the bus turned the corner at the bottom of the street, I was back on my feet.

There was no traffic apart from a set of headlights wavering along the road behind me, going so slowly, whatever it was never drove past.

Down the road and up to the crossroads.

I had two choices here.

I could either go the long way round or take the short

cut across the patch of waste land that ran alongside the playing fields, coming out at the bottom of my street.

On the other side of the wasteland, I knew the bus was climbing the hill because I could hear its engine straining.

So, I took the short cut, setting off at a fast run across the path that led over the waste ground.

I was halfway across when I heard the footsteps behind me and the breathing, so loud, I could hear it above the sound of feet banging onto the snow.

I didn't turn round. I just ran even faster.

Then, a hand grabbed my coat and this sharp smell caught in my throat.

My stilettos were stuffed in my pockets, the ones with long steel spikes for heels, the ones I had worn all day at work, and now I fumbled into a pocket and dragged one shoe out.

It was then that I saw my Dad, turning the corner of the street, head down but marching towards me.

"Dad! Dad!" I yelled.

As my Dad looked up, the sounds behind me stopped and the smell drifted away.

I didn't stop running, didn't even slow down until I reached my Dad.

He started to tell me off.

"I was just coming to meet you. How many times have you been told not to come across the waste land? Then he stopped. "Here," he said. "You don't look very well. You're as white as a sheet."

I didn't tell him about the feet behind me or the sharp spicy smell or the hand which had grabbed at my coat. If I had, I wouldn't have been allowed out on my own again until I was sixty but one thing I did know. I would never ever take a short cut again.

Just as me and my Dad walked through our gate, a car drove past and I looked over my shoulder.

It was covered in snow, so I only caught a glimpse of a face through the driver's side window.

It wasn't a car, though.

It was a van.

That night, I was really poorly and hour after hour, I dreamt that a van was sliding towards me with Mr Grogan behind the steering wheel.

I had mumps.

So did Chuck, which was why he wasn't at the Palais.

"That's what all your kissing has done," Chuck wrote. "!!!!!"

After the mumps, I got bronchitis, then I went down with chicken-pox and then I got better but by that time, the Canadians had gone.

My job at the shop had gone, too.

But I'm not sorry.

I have other plans.

Canada, here I come!

Newts
Pauline Chandler

It was night time at last. Dark and clear: the perfect night. Shivering in the icy twilight, Jean threw back the bedclothes and jumped up. Her bedroom, the narrow box-room at the front of the house, felt damp, as it always did. She rubbed warmth into her arms, then tugged off her thin cotton pyjamas and drew on stiff jeans and a shirt, tucking in her rucked-up vest so there was no cold gap at her back. She was almost ready.

The street lamp winked on, casting a sudden cold light over the room, causing long shadows. Her face in the mirror was a ghost's, wan and pale, but she smiled. There was no point being scared now.

The door creaked noisily as she reached for the denim jacket that hung there. She drew breath and, for a few seconds, held it, still, alert, listening; her pulse acid-sharp. She let go her breath. John was downstairs in the living-room with his girlfriend, Carly. The distant mutter of the television went on without interruption. He hadn't heard the door.

She reached under the bed for her black lace-up school shoes. How she longed for a pair of baseball boots like John's, but Mum had other ideas. She had other shoes: plimsoles and a pair of what Mum called court shoes. They were second-hand, but not a bad fit, her first grown-up pair, black patent leather with Cuban heels. She was supposed to practice wearing them so that she could turn, Cinderella-like, into the grown-up daughter Mum dreamed of. Mum had bought her a pleated skirt, too, and a checked blouse and cardigan, to wear for Sunday best. She must look 'immaculate', that was Mum's word for it, like Aunt Mary's daughter, Alison. *Immaculate*.

But how could you explore and find things out if you had to worry about getting mud on your clothes? She would never be immaculate. Never. Might as well ask a frog to be a butterfly.

She pushed the court shoes aside and pulled out the lace-ups. Wellies would have been the sensible choice, but she didn't have any. Wellies were not immaculate. It was the new school shoes or nothing. She put them on. She was ready. She slung a rucksack over her shoulder and went out on to the landing.

It was the perfect night. Her father was out of the house, at his evening job as barman at the Social Club. Her mother was out too, dancing at the Starlight Ballroom. Neither of them would be back before eleven.

She crept to the top of the stairs, then froze mid-stride as the door to the living-room was flung open. Quick footsteps tapped through the hall into the kitchen. She pushed herself back into the shadows.

Someone went out of the back door. After some minutes, she heard the flush of the outside lavatory next to the coal-house, then the sound of the lavatory door opening and the click of it shutting. Footsteps came back into the house.

She moved to the top step and waited, listening to the sound of water gushing into the kettle. Gas hissed under a ring on the range, then lit with a gasp.

"John? Where's the sugar?"

Carly was making tea. Minutes ticked past. There was a rattle of cups, the ring of spoons, Carly singing a Top Ten tune, quietly, under her breath. Finally, she carried the tea tray to the living-room. Through the banisters, Jean looked down at the top of her head. *If she turned... if she looked up now...*

Carly didn't look up. She pushed open the living-room door and walked inside. The door slammed shut. Jean waited until she heard John and Carly settle to watch TV again, then, slowly, testing every step, she walked downstairs.

The front door opened without a sound as she twisted the snicket of the Yale lock. Squeezing through the narrowest gap, she left the house without looking back, sprinted down the path, through the gate and into the street. The heavy school shoes banged on her heels as she ran. It didn't matter. Nothing mattered. She pumped her arms, pounding the tarmac, filling her lungs with the sweet cold night air.

She had the road to herself. There was no one about — the only movement, as she flew past, was from a flickering TV set in a front room where no one had bothered to draw the curtains. There were no cars. No one saw her. The night was hers.

A street lamp cast its cold glow over Con's front garden. She slipped through the gate, picked up a handful of gravel and threw it up at his bedroom window, which shone with a square of light.

"Con!" She chucked another small scatter of stones and whispered urgently, "Con! Come to the window!"

A shape blocked the light. The window swung open. Con leaned out and looked down.

"Who's that?"

"It's Jean."

"What's up? T'chimney afire or summat?"

"No." She smiled and put her hand to her mouth.

"What do yer want then?"

"Is it dark enough? I've waited for a dark night."

"Yes. It's definitely dark. Well, it *looks* dark. Let me see —" Con pretended to consult his watch. "Oh yeah, that's why — 'cos it's *night* time. 'Course it's dark."

"It's not rainin'."

"No, it's not *rainin'*." Con made a big gesture with his hands, sweeping the night air, feeling for drops of rain, as if he were conducting an orchestra.

Jean laughed and covered her mouth again.

"Are we goin', then?"

"What d'yer mean?"

"To see t'newts. You said you'd take me. It's dark enough, in't it?"

"Aw, 'eck — I can't go now. I've got homework to do."

"You said you'd take me first night, that's what you said. Look, I've brought me collecting jar." Jean pulled a jam jar out of her rucksack. It was four inches in diameter with a wide mouth, and had once held pickles, but she had scrubbed it spotless and tied string round the neck to make a handle.

"Yeah, but I can't come now, I've got work to do."

Jean shoved the jar deep into her rucksack. "I've a tub ready on't back yard to keep 'em in while we study 'em, like you said — zoo-"

"Zoology. Aw 'eck." Con studied the night sky as if to find a message written there. "Where's yer dad?" he said.

"Out at t'club." Jean stared up at Con's white face. "Yer've got to come. I can't go on me own, I don't know where t'pond is, do I? Anyway, I'm stoppin' 'ere until you take me. You promised."

Jean bit down hard on her lip. It had not crossed her mind that Con might not keep his promise, but she wouldn't cry. Her throat grew tight with not crying. She dumped herself down on the damp lawn and gave herself up to a stony silence.

"Aw crike. Hang on then, I'm coming." The window shut abruptly.

She got up, brushed soil from her jeans and wiped her

face on her sleeve, as Con emerged from the house.

"Where's t'net?" she said.

"I'm getting it," Con said, disappearing down the side of the house and returning with a small green pond net on a bamboo cane. "We's'll 'ave to be quick," he said, "I've still got my essay to finish, so make haste."

"Zoo-ology?"

"Yeah."

"Come on then."

Jean struggled to keep up as Con strode ahead. Leaving their road, they walked on down a lane of miners' terraces, through the maze of the council estate and out into the open fields at the edge of the town. All was quiet. There was little traffic and no people about. No one saw them pass.

Jean grinned whenever Con turned to check on her, but she swallowed her excitement. It wouldn't do to giggle out loud like a kid when Con was taking her seriously. He was going to college in September. Leaving home, as she would one day.

They were near the pond. The path threaded its way along the foot of the smouldering slag-heap marking the pit, the coal mine where most people were employed. Dad had already talked about her working there in the offices, if she passed enough exams. He smiled and held her on his knee when he talked about it. It made him happy to plan her future, but she wanted more than an office job.

The sulphurous smell of the slag-heap caught her throat and made her cough. That had happened the first time Con had shown her the ponds, on a summer afternoon when she had come to the fields to collect plant specimens. He had been dipping the pond by himself, looking for specimens of single-celled animals. *Am-amoebae*? She smiled and touched her mouth, pleased to have remembered the correct name.

"You all right, Jean?" Con called back to her.

"Yes," she replied, doggedly following him through the dense patches of nettles and willowherb, eerily blue in the cold glare of the pit floodlights. She shoved aside hawthorn and elder bushes that scratched her face. The pond was a dark eye in the middle. Her feet slipped on the muddy bank.

"Sit there. Don't move until I tell you to. 'Ere." Con passed her the fishing net. "Pass it me when I'm ready."

"Okay, but I want a turn," she said, settling to wait.

Con moved a few yards away, parted the long grass and knelt at the very edge of the water to peer into the depths of the pond.

"We need moonlight. They'll rise to t'surface when t'moon shines on t'water. Keep watching."

"I am."

Jean looked up at the night sky. The moon was there, hidden by thin cloud. It would shine clearly any minute, she was sure it would.

As time passed, she started to feel cold. The backs of her thighs were damp from the wet ground and her breath sat in the air in front of her face, a wavering patch of grey mist. The whole place smelt dank, sour with rotting leaves. The pool was a still black surface. The moon sat stubbornly behind its grey veil. There was no sign of any newts, or anything living in the water at all.

"Can I have a go now?" she called.

Con started at the sound of her voice but did not look up, maintaining his silent vigil.

"I don't think they're rising tonight," he whispered, finally. "I don't think we'll be lucky tonight. I never said we *would* see any. It was only a might and a maybe."

"Let me 'ave a turn."

"All right." With a deep sigh, Con hauled himself to his feet and stepped away from the pond's brink. He passed Jean the net, dripping with a tangle of slimy weed. She took it and held it as if she were a surgeon performing a difficult procedure, lowering the net until the green mesh sat just under the surface. She settled herself to wait.

"We ought to be going soon," Con murmured. "It's getting late. I still have some work to do."

"In a minute," Jean said. The unbroken surface of the pond was a dark mirror reflecting her pale face. She looked like one of those water-nymphs, a *nai-naiad*...

As she remembered the word, the clouds parted and rays of pale moonlight shone down on to the pond. A glowing halo ringed her reflection. A ripple disturbed the image, breaking it apart. *What was that?*

As she stared, a teasing glimpse of gold rolled over the surface of the water, then disappeared.

Con stood up. "I'm goin', Jean. There aren't any tonight."

"I thought I saw one." She kept her eyes on the water.

"Come on — yer just saying that."

She jerked the net from the water and there, in the clear moonlight, was a gleam of greenish gold: a great newt sat at the bottom of the net, smooth olive-green, with a fat golden belly spotted with black. An undulating crest stretched the length of its back.

With an unearthly stare, the newt's golden eye stared back at her, like that of a creature from another world.

"Hah!" Jean shouted. "Look! Look! What a beauty!"

"Great crested! Brilliant! I didn't know there were some in here. Let's see. See that crest down his back? What a beaut'. Great cresteds are quite rare. Where's your jar? Come on, put some water in it, then drop him in. Don't lose 'im. Steady. Right."

Con held the net while Jean half-filled the collecting jar. Carefully, she placed it on the ground. She took the net and held it steady while Con persuaded the newt into the jar.

Jean picked up the jar with both hands and peered at the newt. The newt stared back at her, unblinking. Immobile, it hung like a jewel, suspended, in the clear water.

"You did well," Con said. "Now, have you got 'im? What's the water like in yer tub? You used proper pond water, yeah? It has to be the same as he's used to. You need to lower the jar slowly into the tub, same as I showed you. Let 'im find 'is own way out. Remember?"

Jean nodded. She remembered. Relocating your specimens into an examination tank for close study was a dicey business. You had to be very careful. And be sure to return the specimens to their original *habi- hab-*something, afterwards.

Clutching the precious jar close to her chest, Jean scrambled after Con along the path towards home. Breathless, they reached the top of their road.

"Lower the jar into the water slowly, remember? Don't hurry it," said Con, as they reached his gate. He smiled at Jean. "I'll come down tomorrow after school and we'll do some measuring. Have a notebook ready."

"I will. Then we'll put 'im back. I'll draw him first, though. Bring yer colours."

Con nodded and gestured for her to walk the last stretch of the road alone. It wasn't far to her house. He would watch until he saw her turn safely into her own gate.

"'Bye!" he called.

"See ya!" she replied, her voice shaky with a spurt of sheer joy. Con had looked straight into her eyes. He was talking to her as an equal. She wanted to sprint the last few yards, but she couldn't, not with holding the jar.

As she neared home, John and Carly emerged from a neighbour's house halfway down the road. They came to meet her. In the neighbour's front room, curtains drew aside.

"Where've you been?" John said, his voice pitched high with worry. "We've been searching everywhere! Dad's goin' mad! Do you know what time it is? Nearly midnight! He's waiting for you."

Jean's heart stopped. Her father's anger always stripped her to the bone and left her feeling weak and worn. He had never offered to hit her, though he had strapped John, but he would shout and roar until the house shook, blasting her from wall to wall, watching her shrivel in front of him. She pushed past John and sped down to the house, half-expecting, half-hoping, to see blazing lights, a crowd come to watch, a police car swerving in the gravel, to stop it happening. But there was only the dark night, the cold street lamps and the curious eyes of the neighbours.

She stumbled down the front path and plunged in through the half-open front door. Her father was waiting in the kitchen. At first he didn't speak, but looked at her from under lowering brows.

"Wherever have you been?" The voice was soft to start with, but she knew better than to answer him at this point. All he required was that she stand there and take the brunt. Her eyes flicked to the door into the living-room, which was partly open. Through the narrow gap she could see the edge of her mother's blue dance dress. She was in there waiting for the storm to break and pass. It was what she usually did.

"Answer me!"

Jean glanced back at her dad. *Answer...*

She drew breath and stuck out her chin. "Out with

Con. We've been up to t'pit, to the pond. Catching newts." She held out the collecting jar. Her father didn't look at it. He looked at Jean, studying her face as if she were a stranger who had walked into his house, uninvited.

"Out with Con? Out with CON? What's 'e want wi' you — a great big grown-up lad like that? Out with *CON*? I'll give you 'Out with *CON*'!" He turned to point his finger at her mother, who appeared in the doorway. "If 'e's laid a finger on 'er, I'll smash 'is brains out. OUT WITH CON?" His voice rose to screaming pitch as he paced the room, repeating the phrase, then stopped in front of her again. He poked her hard in the shoulder. She moved back until the table was between them.

"'As 'e touched you? Eh? 'As 'e touched you? *Tell me*! I'll bleddy FLAY 'im!'". As her father reached over to poke her hard in the shoulder again, she felt the collecting jar slip through her fingers until she held it by the string handle, then she swung it across the table. She was aware of an arc of water, then the sound of the impact and breaking glass, then she ran, taking the stairs in twos up to her room, went inside and slammed the door. Great wrenching sobs racked her frame. Heaving violently, she slumped to her knees.

Mrs Carter stood at the kitchen door. Head bowed, she gathered herself and stepped inside. Without looking at him, she walked past her husband and busied herself at the stove, making tea. As she wiped mugs and rinsed the tea pot, he sat, shoulders hunched, staring down at the broken glass and pond water that pooled on the oilskin surface of the table.

"She hit me, Mother." Like a child, he turned and showed her the livid bruise on his temple. "What did she do that for? It were such a whack an' all."

82

There was a long silence, broken only by the hiss of the kettle, which stopped abruptly when Mrs Carter picked it up and poured boiling water on the leaves. After waiting a suitable time for the brew, she poured it out and placed a steaming mug in front of him.

"She's a masterpiece, she is, an' all," he said. Like a conjuror, he laid his two fists on the table. Slowly, he opened his right hand. "She's a mystery. Just look at this beggar."

On the palm of his hand, winking in the bright glare of the unshaded kitchen light, sat the great crested newt.

There was a noise in the hall and he looked up as Jean pushed open the door. As she stepped into the kitchen, he held out his hand, displaying the newt. "What you got 'ere, then, Jean?"

Her dad stared at her. She held out her hand to take the newt.

"I need to put it in water," she said. "There's a tub in the yard. Pondwater. Its proper habitat."

It's a beaut," her dad said, as he looked at his daughter. "A real beauty."

Solstice
Lynne Markham

Here's where I wanted to be: Spain, with Jo and Amy
and the rest. Sprawled on the beach, new bikini (white,
like a retro film star), maybe topless if Ma doesn't get
to see the photos; plugged into my walkman, rock
pounding like canon fire in my ears. Yeah. With nights
spent dancing and dancing, fuelled by warm wine,
exotic food and hot sun making my skin smell like
buttery biscuits baking in the oven. And what else? Oh
yay! Boys, but not the pallid oiks from school, their
pustules blistering in the heat, giggling at bare boobs
like twelve-year-olds with dirty post cards. What I
wanted was smoothness, coolness, the coolness of olive
skin and hair like a crow's wing. Boys who'd been
somewhere, done something, who would know how to
make you feel like you were existing for a time in a
parallel universe compounded of warmth, sea, colours
made brighter by the searing light and wide blue skies.
And sure, maybe I wanted sex if the time was right, the
bloke was right and the whole swirling thing got into
my blood like a mega heart-beat and carried me away.

Here's what I actually got: a week's hiking in the
damp English countryside with Ma and Pa, staying at
one of those centres that specialise in humiliating the
guest. It's Ma who pushes for it, saying stuff like, "It
will be the last time, Fliss, probably our last holiday
together as a family. You've got years ahead of you to go
with your friends. Just think of us for a bit, will you?
Think how we feel, since —" And here's where she
breaks off and assumes a smile that's too obviously
brave, while Pa looks embarrassed in the background

and utters inarticulate noises like a deep gargle at the back of his throat.

What Ma left unsaid was, "since Ali died." Ali was my older sister. She went up to university having done the last holiday stuff with the folks (a canal cruise, yawn, to take in our industrial past) and came back smiling, packed her bags, gave me her second-best jeans and was driven off in a flurry of smiles and kisses and see-you-soons. Only she didn't, of course. Instead, she died of meningitis at the end of her first term, just before the Christmas vacation, and since then there has been a hole in our house, like a deep chasm you could fall into if you weren't looking. It's like teetering on the edge of a precipice and at the bottom of it is Ma's brave smile crumpling her face, fetched up from a sleepless night crying in bed, while Pa tries to comfort her, putting his own feelings on hold and looking at me like he's afraid to let me out of his sight but is too savvy to say so.

It's heavy stuff. I'm their only fragile chick now and it's like I'm living two lives, Ali's and mine, and can't quite get the hang of either of them. So when Ma says, "think of us for a bit", that's a loaded phrase, going deeper and deeper until you feel stifled by it, like, seriously breathless, with this whole lump of emotional weight coagulated into that one deadening phrase.

Right. So that's why I found myself being tipped out of the car and into the sort of place where people say, "Hi! You must be Felicity! Welcome, Felicity. Tea will be served in the lounge in ten minutes' time, and then we will have a short tour of the grounds before our briefing for tomorrow's wonderful walk." It's a place where the staff wear name badges and always remember your own name and use it with irritating regularity. I said, "I'm called Fliss," in a sullen tone that made Ma give me a look that was half annoyed and half tremulous, while

Pa tried to manhandle two suit cases, a weekend bag and two haversacks into the hall without breaking sweat.

The view from my room was wonderful, though. Hills and woods folding down into a broad meadow stuffed with rabbits and swaying grass. At the foot of the furthest hill, a lone stag was grazing peacefully, flanked by lush green trees; a thrush was singing somewhere close by, and if it weren't for the fact that I wanted to be in Spain, that I didn't want to be with Ma and Pa, and that I was seventeen, for God's sake, I would have actually quite enjoyed it. But the tea and the briefing were hell.

The lounge was one of those dreary places you can't imagine sitting in for sheer pleasure. Hard chairs with backs that you can't get your head on, mud-coloured carpet and a book shelf full of books like *The History of Tin Mines in Cornwall* and *Flora and Fauna of the Ex Valley*. Jeez. Most of our fellow-hikers had at least one foot in the grave, glistening white denture smiles and the sort of leathery faces that have been on a hundred hikes too many. Some were already clad in ersatz combat outfits to save on packing, criss-crossed with zips and flapping with pockets whose true purpose escaped me.

I slumped in a chair and folded my arms, scowling, while the wizened Top Dwarf told us about the walk we were to flog off on the next day. Ten flaming miles! No way! I glanced meaningfully at Pa, but he was staring fixedly ahead with the set smile of the polite guest and refused to look at me. So in the end, I got up and walked out, ignoring the dwarf who said, "Are you leaving us, Fliss? Ho ho. Scaring you off already?" and Ma's tight face, already debating whether to come after me or not.

She didn't, and I went outside into air shrill with the

sound of birds: swifts screaming, magpies chattering and that thrush still clamouring from the tip of a tree nearby. I walked along a path skirting the meadow towards a bunch of trees thick with white blossom, scenting the air in that languorous way you get occasionally on warm nights in high summer. In a few days' time it would be the summer equinox, and so the evening was drenched in a veil of pellucid light which seemed to shut out the dark hum of irritation inside my head and be-calm it, as if I was floating on a warm thermal breeze with no particular past or future.

I leaned over a gate and looked out across the meadow at the woodlands falling away into grassland dotted with cows and single trees, like some sepia-coloured eighteenth-century engraving. The trees cast fuzzy shadows and I thought how much Ali would have enjoyed it. I was into music, hip-hop, heavy rock, bands that made your ears jump and thrill, and Ali was the sensitive one. She enjoyed flowers, animals, birds, stuff like that. It's what she was doing at the Uni, botany and the natural sciences. She'd have died for a scene like this.

Yeah. Well.

Well. When I turned to walk back, the moon was up on a parallel with the setting sun and the scene was so perfect, that for a moment I was almost scared. It felt supernaturally still, time out of space, as if the world had stopped abruptly and the past and the future had just fallen away. And then a crow gave a last despairing shriek and the world jerked on again, and I went inside to face Ma and her brave but sad face, and my room with the mud-coloured carpet and the shower too high up on the wall.

I didn't get up for breakfast next day, like, who would at 7am on holiday, for God's sake, in spite of Ma knocking at the door and shouting in whispers through it. I strolled down at nine o'clock when breakfast was cleared away and one of the Dwarves said, "Well, hello there, Fliss. Who's a sleepy-head today?" which I ignored and carried on walking until Ma grabbed my arm and said, "Why aren't you dressed properly? You can't go out like that. Get yourself something to eat from the lunch table and pop upstairs again. We leave at nine-thirty."

"I'm not going." I ambled past her to where the packed lunches were set out on a vast table, all done up in cling film and labelled with the punter's names.

"What? Don't be silly. You can't hang around here all day. Get your things together and we'll be off."

"No," I said loudly, making people look at us discreetly and almost feeling Ali's ghostly presence beside me, willing me to behave, to be kind when I couldn't be, because I felt breathless again, stifled, the wrong daughter in the wrong place. And Ma looking at me with that hurt, baffled look, angry but not showing it. If she'd flaming well *be* angry, let rip at me, come out with a few home truths, I might have gone, but the hurt silence was worse than that, percolating through me so that a kind of dark, sullen obstinacy was the only logical answer to it.

Pa didn't try to persuade me, he just said, "Let her go, Barbara," and to me, "Just be careful, okay?" The sub-text being, we've lost one daughter, the best, and we don't want to lose another, right? And just how likely would that be, statistically speaking? About a zillion to one by my reckoning, so I was statistically as safe as houses, I could go anywhere and do anything and nothing bad would happen to me.

So they went without me, strung out in a long line, haversacks hoisted, maps flapping, calling, "'Bye,

Fliss", with the sort of determined cheerfulness that sets your teeth on edge. After they went I sort of slumped for a bit, relieved and depressed at the same time, conscious that I was failing, not doing my bit to ensure family togetherness, but finally able to breathe properly and spread out inside my own body. Outside, the sun was shining and the scenery seemed to creep up towards the window of the shabby lounge and pull me over towards it. There was a weird feeling of subdued elation gradually seeping through me, which I couldn't pin down to any particular source, just a general idea of expectancy which was vaguely exciting.

I went upstairs and grabbed my bag off the bed, stuffed the lunch into it and went back down, creeping along the hall so the staff didn't notice and Fliss me again. To begin with, I had no idea where I was headed or what I was going to do, there was just this general need to be outside and on my own, away from the main house somewhere. I mooched round the back of the house and passed the swimming pool, still with its plastic cover on, the grass around it dotted with plastic sun-loungers that nobody ever had the time to use. Beyond it there was a narrow track, overgrown with brambles and elder bushes, which terminated suddenly at a dilapidated stile giving entry to a broad meadow. The meadow was lushly grassed and full of buttercups, sweeping up to further meadows dotted with trees and cows I had spotted the previous evening, all overhung by the woods beyond.

I climbed up towards the trees, very slowly, with the sun on my shoulders, hot, but with the rays of light oddly diffuse, as if it was deliberately holding back the full force of its power. My tee-shirt was sticking to me and I was panting slightly, but when I got to the top of the last meadow and turned round to look, I gave a gasp of pure pleasure and hurled myself down on the soft grass and just stared.

Okay. So forget Spain. Forget the sand and the sea. Forget the tepid wine and the boys with the crow's wing hair. For the moment, this was it. Simply the best. I had walked into an idyll and not known how I got there. There was no sound but the buzz of insects, the distant low of a cow, a late cuckoo calling. It was sublime. Nirvana. In that one moment the entire world belonged to me, whizzing through my mind in a dizzying whirl of endless possibilities, and I couldn't even think about Ma and Pa and Ali, or not deliberately, anyway. I mean, Ali's always there, somewhere in my subconscious mind, waiting for me to notice her. But not now. Not at this moment.

I looked for a while longer and then got up to go. I wanted to walk along the edge of the woods and look down through them, over the landscape to the opposite combe where a white church glinted in the sun. But when I turned round and started to walk, I knew immediately that somebody else was there. Not because I could see anybody, but because my internal antennae were naturally sharpened and I could sense another presence getting nearer and nearer. I stopped, and listened. There was a light crack of a twig overlaid by the secret sounds of the countryside. But there it went again: crack, crack.

Just be careful, okay?

My heart gave a loud *whump* in my chest. I thought, so is this when I finally get it? In this place that looks like Paradise but is made of earth and rock and hidden water? Would I die, like Ali? Only not with an illness but with a hammer blow to the head or a knife thrust in the chest? Was that what I secretly wanted, to die like her and be young and beautiful and perfect for ever?

No way.

I would fight for my life like a tom-cat, teeth, nails, no holds barred. But the person who appeared out of the trees looked no older than me. He came down through the woods as if he knew them intimately, not looking where he put his feet but swinging gracefully along, narrowing the distance between us with amazing speed.

"Hi." My arms were folded across my chest and I was scowling again, but more as a programmed response than a true reflection of what I felt. Because this boy was seriously gorgeous, and not in the ordinary way. He was tall and skinny, wearing a dark green camouflage jacket and trousers. His face was very brown, as brown as his hair, with the sort of cheek bones you normally only see on Renaissance portraits in national collections.

"Hi." His teeth glinted in a smile. "You walking my way?"

"Depends." I nodded towards the track following the contours around the edge of the wood. "I'm going that way."

"Good a way as any."

I unfolded my arms and began to shamble along the path, stealing a look at him out of the corner of my eye. He caught the look and held it for a moment, unsmiling. A small ripple of breeze passed over the woods and ruffled my hair. It made my skin crawl briefly into goose-flesh.

"My name's Felicity," I said. "People call me Fliss."

"What are you doing here, Fliss?"

"Holidaying with my folks." I shrugged. "I wanted to go to Spain with my friends, but, you know..."

"Sure. They got to you."

"You know how it is!" I flashed a smile at him. "They want you to go, but they don't. It's kind of..."

"Sad?"

"I was going to say irritating, but sad sort of fits it better. They make you feel responsible for them. Like, if you go away they'll crumple somehow, so you don't go and then you feel mad, like they've got you caught. But now they have, none of you know what to do next. Anyway." I shrugged again. "What are you doing here?"

"I live here."

"God. Lucky you. It's gorgeous."

"Better than Spain, even?"

There was a teasing note in his voice and I shot him another look. His eyes were narrowed, laughing. They were a peculiar hazel colour. Not brown, not green, but somewhere in between, shot through with pin-points of gold.

"Maybe! How do I know? Maybe not. I was going with Jo and Amy. The last fling before we all clear off to different points of the globe. Or at least, to different towns, different colleges. I wanted to swim in the sea, drink the vino, dance the dance." *And meet lots of boys*, but I didn't tell him that, because none of them could be more gorgeous than he was himself, even if he didn't seem particularly aware of it. We were still walking along the track, slightly muddy in parts, with these enchanting views of meadows and church towers dodging in and out of gaps in the field hedge. I stopped to look at one and he stopped with me. There was this smell all around us of warm sun and things growing, the feral smell of high summer, and when he moved, the smell got slightly stronger, like the green smell of nettles.

"You didn't tell me your name," I said.

"Ace."

"Weird! Short for?"

"Just call me Ace."

93

"Right."

We started walking again, quite peaceably, without speaking. By now the sun had shifted slightly in the sky and was angled so that our faces were in the shadows cast by the trees. I had no idea where we were walking to, only that, for some obscure reason, I didn't want the walk to end.

"Look at that." Ace stopped abruptly and pointed through the trees. To begin with I couldn't see anything, but then I made out the triangular face of a fallow deer peering through a fringe of leaves.

"Jeez," I whispered, without thinking, "Ali would have loved that."

"Ali?"

When it heard our voices, the deer melted away silently into the tree cover, and Ace turned towards me, his hazel eyes masked by the fall of the pattern of leaves.

"My sister," I said, awkwardly, because, damn it, she was on my mind when I didn't want her to be, when I wanted to be free of her, to be myself, to feel the moment, to go with it wherever it decided to take me.

Ace carried on looking at me in silence, just waiting, until I began to feel — not scared, exactly, but apprehensive, as if I was getting deeper and deeper into something I couldn't escape from.

"She died," I said shortly. "Two years ago. She loved this sort of stuff. Nature. Trees, flowers. You know. That was her. She was a bit like a flower herself. Laughing. Open. A summer flower. God, I'm sorry."

Tears were starting at the backs of my eyes and I fumbled for a hanky but couldn't find one, so dabbed about with the bottom of my shirt, while Ace carried on waiting, his gaze now turned onto the path which disappeared round a bend in front of us.

"Sometimes I hate her!" I blurted out. "I hate her for dying, for always being one step ahead of me. For not living long enough to be a nuisance, to fail or make mistakes. To grow old and ugly. I hate her for leaving me behind!"

The wind rustled in the trees, and I applied the shirt to my sodden eyes and streaming nose while Ace began to walk on very slowly and quietly. When I caught up with him, the warmth and the soft breeze seemed to blot the words out, as if they were absorbed into the green hollow of the high noon and somehow made less awful.

"Sorry," I said. "I'm okay now." We were standing at another bend in the track and Ace waited while I sorted myself, smoothing my hair, pulling my shirt down, hitching the bag up on my shoulder. Then he pointed down a field at right angles to the track.

"This is where we part. If you turn down that track and carry on in a straight line, you'll see the path back to the house. You'll be fine now."

"What? Sure. Okay." It irritated me that I was leaving him with this image of me with a tear-sodden, swollen face and snot on the edge of my shirt, but short of hanging on to him, which would be just too uncool, there was no way to stop it.

"Good-bye, Fliss." Ace began to turn back onto the track and before I could stop myself, I said, too quickly,

"'Bye. Shall I... will you... I mean. Will you be here again? I mean, like, any time this week? Tomorrow or whenever?"

A twig cracked in the undergrowth, disturbed by some small animal, and it seemed suddenly cooler, although the sun still shone. Ace paused for a moment and looked at me, his face half-hidden in the tree shadows. "We'll see each other again, Fliss. I promise you." And an accident of light made it look as if leaves were tumbling out of his mouth with each word and shooting up to form a wavy green aura around his head. He raised his hand to me and turned away, and I followed the track he had pointed out through the singing green meadows, all the way back to the house. It was only when I got there that I thought, how did Ace know where I was headed? At no time had I said where I was staying. So maybe it was simply local knowledge, maybe it was just a lucky guess.

When Ma and Pa got back later they seemed better, more relaxed, as if the ten-mile trek had ironed out the kinks in their psyche and they were less uptight and irritable. Ma even managed a jolly smile, "Had a good day, Fliss? What did you get up to? Nothing too wicked, I hope?"

"It was okay," I shrugged. "I did this and that. Nothing special. Just — you know."

"Well, you look better for it, anyway." Ma inspected me more closely and I glanced away, irritated and embarrassed, because it was true what she said: I did look better. When I caught sight of myself in the mirror behind her, my face looked weirdly fuller, like it had somehow unfolded and become softer and less tense. Even my hair seemed to be wavier and was falling to my shoulders in loose clumps. But there was no time to look properly, or to think about it, because dinner was served and after that there was a de-briefing, during which time I skulked silently in a corner of the lounge, flicking through the pages of *The Tin Mines of Cornwall* and ignoring shots aimed at me by the eager-beaver dwarves and dwarfesses.

What interested me, though, was talk about the solstice. Apparently, some of the locals got together at Midsummer's Eve and toured the villages and hamlets, inviting people to dance. "It's great fun, but you need to be careful," one of the leaders said, "it can get a bit wild. It's kind of.. primitive, I guess. The men wear horns and so on. Some of them wear masks. They usually call here, but they don't get many takers. Too old for 'em, I reckon — but you'd better watch yourself, Fliss! Young girl like you. Just the ticket, I'd say!"

I blushed scarlet and stared furiously at a picture of a miner with a beard and long clay pipe, while Ma and Pa laughed politely and pretended not to be alarmed.

The next day they were even crosser when I wouldn't go out with them. "What will you do all day?" they asked, secretly imagining men in antlers, probably with cloven feet, whisking me off in broad daylight while they fearlessly trekked the Valley of the Rocks.

"Dunno," I shrugged. "Stay here, probably."

But I was lying, because what I intended to do was walk the woods and meadows again, hoping that Ace would appear, remembering what he said, *We'll see each other again, Fliss. I promise you*, knowing that he was the sort of man who kept his promises.

I set off as soon as the walkers disappeared round the corner, led by one of the Chief Dwarves who called out, "Watch yourself, Fliss! You're in wild country here!" and then had to contend with Ma saying distractedly, "Do you think we should leave her on her own? P'raps one of us should go back," and was laughed down by the dwarf's cohorts, who mistook her fretting for jokiness.

It was hotter than the day before, the sky almost bleached of colour by the high sun, a pale gossamer haze smoking over the grass and trees and blurring their shapes. I walked the same path I had walked yesterday, and then carried on along it to a forked track leading to the next village a couple of miles away. I met

97

no one, but all around me the chattering sounds of invisible life carried on, made sharper and clearer by ears which were straining for the crack of a twig, the rustle of a leaf, anything which would herald the sudden arrival of Ace. But he didn't come. The morning and afternoon passed by in a gentle haze, broken only by shafts of sun glinting like spears on the ground, and in the middle of the afternoon I slept deeply in the shade of a hawthorn tree, and then trailed back to the house, my skin burnt by the sun and conscious of an odd feeling of displacement, as if a fundamental change was taking place inside me and I had no power to stop it.

After dinner, the briefing and de-briefing. After that the Bright Sea Lady Hand-Bell Ringers playing 'I'm called Little Buttercup' with unconscious and hilarious syncopation.

Next day I wandered off again, hoping against hope that I would see Ace, Ma and Pa no longer bothering to persuade me to go with them. "Just be careful," they said, eagerly stepping out in their sensible shirts and trousers, water bottles bobbing at their hips. It struck me that they, too, seemed curiously flattened and laid-back, as if suspended in some kind of dreamy time-warp where the world was beautiful, and the terrible thing with Ali had never happened.

But I didn't want to be careful, I wanted Ace, and he failed to materialise again, either that day or the following day, until I began to doubt whether I had actually met him at all. I thought maybe it was just a trick of the light, or a figment of my imagination, that I was unconsciously compensating myself for the loss of the olive-skinned Adonises with crow's wing hair and knowing faces.

By Midsummer's Day, the sun was at its highest point in the sky. The day was hot and still and cloudless. Birds were still swooping and screaming at eleven o'clock at night and the fields and woods and meadows seemed to unfurl and open towards the sun like a fist slowly unclenching. After dinner, the talk was all of dancing, of the deer-men who would visit when the moon was up and before the sun had sunk in the sky.

Pa said, "There's games in the lounge tonight, pet. I think you should join us." The sub-text being, no local louts are going to get their hands on my daughter! It made me laugh, but I wanted to cry as well, and I shrugged him off and went outside to lean over a gate and watch the light changing over the distant hills.

I didn't hear the dancers arrive. They must have come silently through the slowly darkening night to arrive at a point behind me, already done up in their masks and antlers and looking oddly frightening: too ferociously real, like some picture from a book on Greek mythology, come to life.

"Join the dance, lady?" the nearest dancer spoke to me in a deep burr, holding his hand out invitingly, backed up by the others, boys, men, women and girls, all garlanded with leaves and flowers. I stepped forward, and then hesitated for a moment. *Just be careful. Okay?* Beyond the single lantern they carried, the night now seemed infinitely darker and more impenetrable than it had only a minute before. The moon hung like a flat disc over the woods and there was that feral smell again, wild and hungry, which made me put my hand in his.

"Sure," I said, and the music started up, just a piper and a drum, but the beat they gave out was mesmerising, so that once you heard it and started to dance, you had to keep on dancing and dancing while the moon glittered and the stars hurled down dazzling shards of light onto the earth below.

The man's hand felt soft and dry, silky, like the underside of a leaf. He wasn't wearing antlers, but his head was wreathed with a garland of leaves, his eyes masked by the glancing shadows from them. When we danced, the beat of the music seemed to be absorbed into us. The heat of the day, the lushness of the meadows, bird song, flowers like jewels in the mind, all mutated into music, absorbed into our skin, into our bones, into our minds. I tried to pull away, to slow things down, but the man's grip on me was too tight and too fierce.

"Don't be afraid," he said. The words erupted from his mouth in a shower of leaves which cloaked his shoulders and leapt around his head, weaving a living crown of green which, even as I looked, burst into blossom and shone brighter and clearer than the fizzing stars.

"Ace," I said, breathlessly, "it's you, isn't it? It *is* you."

The man didn't answer, but simply spun me round in the dance until I felt dizzy and disorientated, the night a whirling mass of shapes and images, which resolved themselves finally into a deep hollow of darkness.

As suddenly as we began dancing, we stopped, and the man said softly, "Look, now. And listen." We were still holding hands, and when he let go it was like letting go of a terrible grief, a loss too great and too profound to cry over. For a long moment, the earth seemed to tilt and spin while the music faded and the night took on its own shape again, inch by inch, the trees appearing like smoke shadows against the luminous midnight sky.

"Ali?" I said, cautiously. But there was no reply, just a faint rustle of leaves where the breeze caught them and this creeping feeling of lightness, like a silk scarf floating in the breeze.

Ali! Ali! Ali!

The words crowded back inside my head; the grass was cool under my feet, and where the moon shone you could see buttercups glinting, tinged with silver.

I said softly, "I'm going, Ali. But you know that, don't you?"

It was deeply still. Where the sun had left the sky there was a single, faint finger of gold. I put my hands to my head. *Look. And listen.* If I wanted to, I could see Ali, because she was everywhere. She was in every blade of grass and every flower and leaf. She was in my music and in my blood and in my bones. Two in one. Just me. Just my life to live. The almost unbearable lightness of it.

I wandered down the path towards the house and it felt as if I was floating above the ground. There was no sign of the dancers and the house was lit up like a ship at anchor. Some people were clustered round the door, presumably looking for the dancers and the piper, and the drummer who side-kicked with every alternate beat of the drum.

The Chief Dwarf caught sight of me. "Hey, Fliss!" he said. "Been looking for the dancers? Hard luck. They don't come here every year. I guess we were just unlucky this time."

I shook my head and strolled past him and went up to my room. The window was open and I leaned out. In a peculiar freak of moonlight I could see a solitary deer gazing towards me, motionless in the lea of the hills. I stared back at it, and then drew the curtains slowly across the dark glass. It was late and I was tired. I thought I had better go to bed, because in the morning I had a long way to go.

Strawberry Wine (extract)
Berlie Doherty

My mum was only on the first day of her five-day holiday in the Lakes when my adventure started. It was the first time she'd left me on my own. It will probably be the last.

She left just after breakfast. It was too early for my bus to school, so I decided to walk over to my girlfriend's house and catch it with her. Nobody knew she was my girlfriend, not even Caroline. This week would probably help to change all that. Her mum and mine were close friends, and I'd known Caroline for years, even before we moved to Edale. And suddenly she was beautiful. How come I'd never noticed it before? How come her smile turned my bones to water?

So I set off with plenty of time to spare. The road was still quiet. The early workers had gone into Sheffield or wherever, the tourists hadn't started flooding in. Apart from the drone of a tractor and the bleating of the sheep, the valley was silent. I love it like that. It was already hot, the September sky just about as blue as it could get. I gazed up at it, trying to remember whether Caroline's eyes were blue, and practising how I could tell her that they looked like the sky. Windows of the sky. Pools reflecting the sky.

It made me dizzy, so I looked down, and saw a purse on the road. Funny, how you get those prickly feelings, sure that someone's watching you. But there was no-one in sight. I picked the purse up and opened it, feeling furtive and guilty as I did so. A quick glance showed me that there was about a hundred pounds in notes, and quite a bulge of coins in the zip bit. No credit cards. A

Derbyshire library card. I flipped it over. The signature was hard to read. Win Lingworth. The name sounded familiar, but I couldn't put a face to it. I had a feeling that was the name of the woman who lived by the railway cuttings — we called it the hidden cottage because it couldn't be seen from the road or the train, you had to know it was there.

I prised my fingers down inside another of the pockets. There was a 'cardiac alert' card, with an emergency number to call in case of a heart attack. That made me feel a bit strange, as if I knew a secret about somebody. A few receipts, two books of stamps. I looked round again, hoping that whoever had dropped it would come running back for it. Well, not running if they were about to suffer a heart attack. There was still no-one, but still that strange sensation that I wasn't on my own.

I had several options now. I could keep the purse. Against my principles. I could keep some of the notes. Again, not my kind of thing. I could report the find to the police. That might mean having to trail into Sheffield or something. What a waste of a day. I could leave it where I'd found it. She might come back looking for it any minute. But someone else might find it who didn't have the same principles as me. Or I could return it myself.

If she did live in that hidden cottage, it was hardly out of my way. I had to pass the end of the lane on my way to Caroline's and I still had plenty of time to spare. It would be my good deed for the day. It would be something to tell Caroline about. It might impress her.

I set off at a jog and swung into the little lane that the hidden cottage shared with a farm. There were two wheelie bins and two mail boxes at the end of the lane, really the only things that showed that there was any habitation down there. After about half a mile, the lane split into two tracks. One of them snaked off to the left, and the other deeply rutted track swung off to the right and down into a shady hollow. I was confused; I'd never been down either way before, and I couldn't think which would be more likely. I decided to take the left-hand one, which looked better used. I came to a rickety five-bar gate with a broken hinge, and lifted it open carefully.

"Where d'you think you're going?" a man's voice bellowed across the field, and I retreated rapidly. A thick-set, scowling farmer approached me with a dog with a hundred teeth, snarling at his side.

"Sorry, I've come the wrong way," I shouted over my shoulder. What you learn round here is, some farmers are nice, some aren't, and they're all utterly charming when they think you're trespassing on their property.

I glanced at my watch. Still loads of time. I ran back to the other track which soon plunged down into a densely canopied hollow. The cottage was much further than I expected, if there was anything there at all, and I was just beginning to think I'd gone completely wrong when I saw a woman's yellow cardigan or jacket of some sort lying in a big clump of nettles. It was humped over in a strange, bulky sort of way.

I felt a bit queasy, seeing that. There was no way I was going to put my hand in the clump for it, even if they hadn't been stinging nettles. What if someone was still wearing it? What if she'd realised that she'd lost her purse and had a cardiac arrest? I worked my way round the clump and made quite sure it was just an empty jacket, then I found a branch lying on the ground and hooked the jacket up with it. It was quite light, with a weight of some sort in one of the pockets. I put my hand inside. It was a mobile phone.

If this belongs to Win Lingworth too, then she must be pretty careless, I thought, losing a purse and a jacket and phone on the same day. It could hardly belong to anyone else. I couldn't imagine who might come up here, it was so overgrown. Well, I put the jacket over my arm and carried it up the track, and was very relieved when I saw the gate of the hidden cottage. Hooked over the post was a pair of binoculars.

She's mad, I thought. She'd lose her head if it was loose, Mum would say.

I left them where they were, this time. She could find those for herself. The gate was standing open, but there were so many weeds pushing up around it that I doubt if it was ever closed. I went on up the twisty path to the front door. That was open too.

I knocked loudly. "Miss Lingworth!" I shouted. "Miss Lingworth!"

The silence was like a waiting breath. I could hear my own heart beating into it. I went round to the back of the house. It was a jungle of weeds and flowers struggling together for light. There was the scorched remains of what must have been quite a large bonfire. A vegetable patch had almost gone to seed, but for a row of straggly potato plants. The leaves hung long and heavy, with a few yellow flowers still glowing on the ends of the trailing stalks. Butterflies danced everywhere as if it was their Paradise. At the bottom of the garden was a large pond, the nearest edge strangely cleared of the dense jumble of weeds that clogged up the middle. A few lilies as white as little clouds sat on the dark water. And again, that deep, deep silence, except for the heavy droning and whining of insects.

I turned back towards the house and saw that the kitchen door was open. She must be there. I hammered on it as loudly as I could, shouting her name, and when

I stopped, the memory of my voice hung scared and strangled in the humming silence.

I stepped into the kitchen and put the jacket and the phone and purse on the table. Bluebottles buzzed round me. I turned and ran down the lane, ran all the way to Caroline's, and just missed the bus.

Nothing is more annoying than missing the Bakewell bus. There's only one a day from here, taking all the older kids in the valley (about six of us) to school. I'd never even gone that way before, as I'd only started at that school that term. All the Year Elevens had to go to either Bakewell or Sheffield; miles away, both of them. I knew it meant that I had to walk all the way to Edale station, wait forty minutes, then wait another half-hour for a bus to take me to Bakewell. What a pain!

By the time I arrived at school it was the end of break, I was in trouble, and I'd missed the chance of seeing Caroline. But none of that was as bad as the nagging sense of unease I felt all day about Win Lingworth.

The more I thought about her, the better I remembered her; a white-haired, clever-looking little woman. I had first seen her on the station platform, pacing up and down when Mum and I were waiting for the train one day. It was a few years ago, we hadn't lived in Edale very long, and Mum was anxious to get to know people in the valley.

"Are you local?" Mum asked.

"I am." She had answered rather stiffly, as if she resented the intrusion into her silence. Mum said later that she thought it was shyness, but then, Mum always thinks the best of everyone.

"Ah, I'm pleased to meet you. I'm Barbara Neild, and this is my son, Shaun. So hard to get to know people. You are — ?"

"Win Lingworth." She treated Mum to a surprisingly sweet smile, then edged away as if she was peering to see if the train was coming through the distant tunnel. One light means it'll stop here, two means it's the express from Manchester to Sheffield.

"Off to Sheffield?" Oh, Mum is so nosy when she's trying to be friendly.

Miss Lingworth took a deep breath, resigning herself to conversation. "I'm going to London."

"Nice."

"I hate London."

"It can be a bit scary, but you have to go sometimes."

"I have a business appointment with my research assistant."

"Oh?" Mum's question marks throbbed in the air like little dragonflies, and at last Miss Lingworth satisfied her.

"I'm a writer," giving the briefest smile this time. Then she tilted her glasses at Mum, putting a final glassy barrier between them; a 'Don't ask me anything else' sort of look, and moved off to the other end of the platform.

Mum couldn't wait to find out more. She phoned one of her friends, Sandra, who used to be headmistress of the village primary school and knew just about everybody, and found that Win Lingworth lived somewhere near the railway cutting down our end of the valley. That evening she took Buster for a walk down there, just for a look. Mum calls it getting to know the neighbourhood. I call it spying.

"Lovely old cottage, gorgeous garden. Very secluded," she told me later. "I wouldn't choose to live there, not on my own."

So, anyway, all I knew about Win Lingworth was that she was a writer. Not very successful, by the look of her dowdy little cottage. It didn't quite fit Mum's description of it, anyway.

I fretted about her most of the evening. I think that cheerful greeting from the farmer must have unnerved me, which was why I'd been so jittery at the cottage. There was nothing to watch on telly and my DVDs had all become boring, so I brought my bike in and took it to bits on the kitchen floor, which Mum would have loved. She rang up to see how I was getting on without her and Buster, and I told her I hadn't even noticed they weren't in the house. I looked round happily at the dissected bike on the floor.

Then, because she was obviously on the point of asking whether I'd had a good day at school, I told her about the purse and the jacket and the empty cottage.

"She's probably just gone for a stroll," Mum said. "I'd give her a ring, Shaun. She'll be in the phone book. Just let her know you called."

It was a good idea, but it didn't help at all. It made things worse. The phone rang for ages, and I was just about to give up when she picked up the receiver. Either that or the ansaphone clicked on, it was hard to tell. Either way, no one spoke. Not a word. But I was sure I could hear someone breathing, very light, very quick, at the other end.

"Miss Lingworth," I said. "Miss Lingworth, are you there? It's Shaun Neild. I think I found some of your things —"

Nothing.

I felt silly, talking to nothing. And I felt a bit scared too. So I put the phone down and stared at it for about ten minutes, then went to bed.

But I didn't sleep. What if it was Miss Lingworth on the other end, but she was too ill to speak? Maybe I should ring the police. But it sounded feeble. Someone didn't answer the door. Someone didn't answer when I spoke. So what?

She's a recluse, I told myself at last. She likes her privacy. She has a right to her privacy.

And I fell into an uneasy sleep.

As soon as I woke up the next morning I knew I would have to go back to the hidden cottage. I would say I wanted to make sure that the things I had found belonged to her. That was fair enough — if they weren't hers, they would have to be reported to the police. So, quite confidently this time, I set off for the lane by the cuttings. Just where the two tracks forked, I saw a woman bending over some bushes. She looked up sharply as I drew alongside her, as if she'd been concentrating on something and I'd made her jump out of her skin. She obviously wasn't expecting anyone to come down that lane. He lips were purple blotches in a white, startled face.

"Oops," she said, smiling garishly. "Oh, it's only you, Shaun."

I stared at her, hesitating for a moment. It's unnerving in this valley, how all the adults seem to know all the kids. They all come to the primary school play, and there's never more than twenty-two children in the school. Mind you, there's not that much else in the way of entertainment. Anyway, I just treated her to my best 'fancy seeing you here' smile. She picked up a bag and scuttled away from me, whistling carelessly. But it wasn't Win Lingworth, I knew that, at least. It was someone from the mill cottages, though I hadn't a clue what her name was. I jogged on down the shadowy track and through the gate. The binoculars were still there. Again, the front door was open. Again, I called and knocked. Again, no answer.

I went round the back. I tried the kitchen door. It was open. I knocked and called, and again there was no answer. I took a deep breath, and stepped inside. It was a dark little kitchen, with a big black old-fashioned fireplace. The jacket and purse and phone lay on the table, exactly where I had left them. My heart was knocking in my chest now. Something was wrong, something was desperately wrong. I would have to search the house for her. But the thought of going through the rooms, climbing the stairs, opening doors into private rooms, and finding — what? a dead woman slumped over a telephone? — it was all more than I could handle. Perhaps I should look round the garden first, then knock again, and then go away and phone the police. They could do the searching; that was their job, they were used to it.

I went back out into the garden, and there she was, standing in the middle of the overgrown veg. patch, digging potatoes. How come I hadn't seen her before?

"Hello there!" she called. "Was it you who brought my things back? Very kind of you."

She bustled towards me, dimpling with smiles, and I nearly hugged her, I was so relieved.

"You've helped me a great deal, young man, more than you think," she said, pulling off her gardening gloves. Her hands had those little brown blotches that old people get. She took off her glasses and blew a speck of soil off the lens. "Ha! Can see you now. Come inside and have a cup of tea."

Of course I was overjoyed by her kind invitation, but luckily I had a good excuse. "I need to get off and catch the bus," I told her. "I just wanted to make sure —" It sounded silly now, but she finished the question off for me.

"That I'm still alive? Well, I am, as you can see.

111

Sorry to put you to so much trouble, but you've very kindly helped me in a bit of research. I'm writing a bit of a thriller at the moment, a murder mystery, just a silly amateur thing, I like to do a bit of scribbling. I laid a bit of a trap for you, I'm afraid. Just wanted to see what would happen if someone found a purse and a jacket and an empty house. I can move on to the next bit, now. Very exciting! I might make you one of the characters!"

She beamed at me so cheerfully that it was hard to be angry with her, but my relief had turned to embarrassment and a slight annoyance. I thought she'd made a fool of me, and now I just wanted to get away, and turned to move off.

"Wait a minute," she called. "I want to give you something for your honesty and your help." She dived into the kitchen.

"No, I really don't want anything," I called. "I'd better be off."

She emerged quickly with a bottle of something pink. "Strawberry wine," she said. "You're old enough to drink wine, I'm sure. It's home-made, and it's the last one. Beautiful, isn't it? Look at the colour." She held it up so the sun was shining through it, a gorgeous pale glow like roses. She held it out to me. "Take it," she said, "with my sincere thanks."

"Thank you." I hate wine, but I was too embarrassed to say so. I stuffed it awkwardly into my school-bag and turned away.

"Make sure you drink it all yourself!" she called. "And come back to see me any time you like!"

I ran for the bus, the wine slurping in its bottle. I would show it to Caroline, I promised myself. I'd invite her round, and we'd share it. And then, oh bliss, and then —

I missed the bus. And German, which was the only lesson I shared with Caroline. I didn't see her to speak to all day, but I did notice her chatting to Tom Butcher at lunch time. He lives in Edale, he's over a year older than me, he's probably the best-looking kid in school, and he's just passed his driving test. First time. Well, I like Tom, everyone does, but I felt so annoyed with him for the way Caroline was glowing at him that I wanted to trip him up when he walked past. In Edale, the farm kids learn to drive when they're about ten, charging up and down the fields on massive tractors or quads, rounding up the sheep. The rest of the kids start learning on their seventeenth birthday, on the dot, so their parents have to stop ferrying them round the county, which is an awful disappointment to them but they learn to do without it.

So, back home to my bike bits. Someone had left a carton of eggs on the doorstep, without a note, but I assumed Mum had asked Robert, the farmer next door, to deliver them. I decided to make an omelette. The house was so loud with the silence of no Mum and no Buster that I put on a CD at maximum volume, sang my head off, and danced over the bike bits while I chopped several onions and a bit of cauliflower into the omelette, burned it, scrambled it, and finally scraped it onto a plate. The inside of the frying pan looked like a totally brilliant piece of abstract art.

The music was so loud that I hardly heard the phone when it rang. It was someone asking if I'd enjoyed the eggs and had I by any chance found something or other that I couldn't hear. We shouted at each other for a bit, and then whoever it was put down the receiver. The CD stopped, I finished my egg mess, put the abstract art in the sink, and the long silent evening stretched in front of me like a prison sentence.

I didn't see Caroline again till next day. I managed to sit behind her on the bus, and to my joy she actually turned round to speak to me.

Yes, her eyes are blue.

"I've got some German notes for you, but I've left them at home." My chance had come, and I grabbed it with grateful hands.

"Could you bring them round tonight?" I asked innocently. "I'd come round to yours, but I've got to wait for a phone call from Mum." That was true, but there was nothing wrong with our ansaphone. She gave me one of those bone-melting smiles and whispered something to the girl sitting next to her, and I rode on a cloud all the way to school.

When I got home that night, I pushed the bike bits under the kitchen table, scrubbed the abstract art and sorted out some good CDs. I put the bottle of strawberry wine on the kitchen windowsill with the light behind it. Caroline noticed it as soon as she came in.

"It's so beautiful," she said. "As if the sunset is inside it."

"I want to share it with you," I said. "Shall we have some now?" My hand was reaching for the corkscrew, and shaking a little. My mind was already thinking about later, later. But she smiled and shook her head.

"I can't," she said. "Mum's waiting outside for me. We're going to Sheffield to the library."

I must have looked as crest-fallen as I felt, because she put the German notes on the table and then touched my hand, lightly and shyly, and I felt delicious electric shocks running up and down me. And then the phone rang, and my mum was on for ages, raving about the fact that she'd just seen a herd of wild deer, and then Caroline's mum was hooting outside the gate...

"Come with us," Caroline said. "Pretend you've got to go to the library too."

I'd have gone with her if she'd been driving to the rubbish tip.

It was while I was waiting for her and her mother to come out of the library, that I saw Win Lingworth again. She was crossing the road to the underpass that led to the Odeon. I raised my hand to wave to her but she didn't see me, or didn't want to see me. She was hurrying, and her face looked grim, and white, and ugly. And there was definitely something different about her, but I couldn't put my finger on it. It wasn't just her expression, either. It made me feel cold with unease. Caroline came out of the library just then, and I pointed her out.

"There's Win Lingworth," I said. "From the hidden cottage."

Caroline shook her head. "I don't think that's her," she said. "Win's hair's different, I'm sure. Thicker than that."

"So you know her?"

"Mum does, a bit," Caroline said. "She pointed her out to me a few weeks ago. I don't think anyone knows her very well. She doesn't mix. But I'm sure that's not her."

So, I was mistaken. I told her and her mum the story about the strawberry wine anyway, when we were driving back home. Her mother was very amused.

"I'm pleased to know she's turning to thrillers," she said. "She writes very stuffy books about international politics. Sandra and I looked her up on the Internet one day. Very high up in her field, by all accounts."

"The strawberry wine's still waiting," I whispered to Caroline as I climbed out of the car at our gate. "How about tomorrow?"

She just shook her head and gave me a smile that was half-rueful and half-teasing. "Away," she mouthed.

I found out when I was on the school bus next morning that Caroline was on a field trip, staying overnight on a camp site somewhere near Stanton Moor. Lucky campers, lucky tent, lucky sleeping bag. I was as miserable as old boots all day. It was my last chance of having that evening of bliss. When I got home, the house was empty and quiet; no Mum, no Buster, no Caroline. I took Miss Lingworth's bottle of strawberry wine and held it up to the light. I could hear Caroline's voice saying, "It's got the sunset inside it."

I would drink to that, I decided. I would drink to me and Caroline, and the sunset; I would drown my sorrows. I fished around for the corkscrew and was about to open the bottle, when I realised what a saddo I would be, drinking on my own, drinking wine, of all things, which I love about as much as vinegar without the chips. I put the bottle back on the windowsill. I'd give it to Mum tomorrow. That's what I'd do. A welcome home present.

I went out for a run instead. I couldn't resist jogging down to Miss Lingworth's. The oldest woman in Edale tooted the horn of her Fiesta at me, just by the two wheelie bins at the end of the lane. That's another thing about driving in Edale. Not only can you start when you're ten but you can carry on till you're ninety-four. She peered at me and wound down her window, driving alongside me as I was running, and dangerously close.

"Want any more eggs?" she asked.

Ah, so it was her. "No thanks, Milly. Still cleaning the pan," I puffed.

"I'm still looking for my whatsits! Such a nuisance!

116

Can't manage without them." She swerved round a crow that was tugging a rabbit carcass off the road, and I jammed myself into the hedge, just managing to save my life. I smiled gratefully at her as she careered on her way.

I plunged down into the safety of Miss Lingworth's track. If I saw her, I'd thank her for the wine. I'd tell her it was delicious. I'd ask her how her thriller was coming on. I stopped at the gate, panting, noting that she'd retrieved the binoculars at last. It was quite late, the bats were out in search of midges. The drone of insects was as heavy as a distant rumble of thunder. And apart from that, silence; utter, utter silence. An open door, a silent, empty house, and a day breathing towards night. Long grey shadows. I have never felt so afraid in my life.

After that, I couldn't wait for Mum and Buster to come home. I'd had enough of being on my own. It was turning my imagination loopy. If only Caroline hadn't been away on that field trip, we could have made great progress. As it was, I wrote letters to her, text messages, phone calls, none of which got sent as I had no idea where she was anyway, or what her mobile number was. And mobiles don't work at our end of Edale. She could have phoned me, but she didn't. I couldn't get her smile, or the sound of her voice, or the blue sky of her eyes out of my mind. She was haunting me.

As soon as I heard Mum's car, I was out in the lane, waving to her. She was as pleased to see me as I was to see her. Buster came leaping out of the car and licked me all over as if I needed a bath, then bounced into the kitchen and nearly knocked over the bottle of strawberry wine off the table. I rescued it just in time, and handed it to Mum.

"Welcome home."

"How lovely!" Mum said. "What an amazing colour. Strawberry wine!"

I held it up so she could see the light shining through it. "It looks as if it's got the sunset inside it." It sounded a bit pompous when I said it. I whisked two glasses out of the cupboard. "Let's have some now."

"No, not just yet," she said. "I really could do with a walk, and so could Buster, after that long drive. You could make a bicycle out of those bits under the table, by the way. Come with me and tell me all the news, and when we come back, we'll open the bottle and celebrate."

But the bottle was never opened, thanks to Mum's curiosity and Buster's passion for water.

As we walked, I told Mum about Win Lingworth — well, it was the only news I had. Mum was fascinated.

"Let's go there now," she said. "I'd love to meet her properly."

"She hides," I warned her. "There's something really strange about that place. It's so quiet. It's spooky."

"She needs friends, that's all. It's too easy to be isolated here, you have to work at it if you want to meet people. I know what I'll do. I'll ask her if she'd like to donate a couple of bottles of her beautiful wine to the local products stall at the Autumn Fair."

"It's her last bottle," I argued weakly. I knew Mum wouldn't give up now she knew that Miss Lingworth was writing a thriller, especially as I was going to have a star part in it. It made her a bit more interesting. Political analysis wasn't quite Mum's thing. I wasn't even sure what it meant myself.

"I could invite her to give a talk at the WI." Mum confirmed my suspicions absolutely. "We haven't had a writer for a few years."

118

Buster lolloped ahead of us up the lane, and then stopped suddenly, snarling and crouching in a strange, cowed way. He didn't want to go any further, and to tell the truth, neither did I. And we arrived to the same eerie stillness, the open front door, the open kitchen door, the jacket and purse still on the table, the terrible ceaseless droning of flies. And then Buster noticed the pond and flung himself straight in, and disturbed what I thought, from the distance of the kitchen, was a dark jumble of weeds.

No, it wasn't.

It was a body.

It was Win Lingworth.

Thaw
Bette Paul

February in the Pennines is like three in the morning —
life's lowest ebb. It's the cold heart of winter up here —
fog, frost, snow interspersed with bouts of stormy winds
and driving rain. And never really light. Dad calls it 'the
long, dark night of the soul', and I was so depressed
that a dose of self-flagellation would have come as light
relief.

The half-term holiday didn't help — I'd a mountain
of work to shift before exams and nobody had time to
help. Dad was watching over the spiritual needs of
three parishes and Mum was fighting off the 'flu
epidemic down at the so-called Health Clinic, a bit of an
oxymoron just then. So I was left to get on with my
work alone. Nothing new in that; I'd spent most of my
childhood alone — vicarage children often do.

Not that I minded; for years I'd been too busy
working towards the Great Escape, to worry about
being lonely. My school reports were good, projected
exam grades excellent, references impeccable, and now
I was on the last lap. All I needed were a few decent
results and I could leave Thorneywood behind. It was
those final results that were causing all the trouble: I
was working hard, but I couldn't seem to absorb
anything. Hour after hour, page after page, and then —
blank! Just at the most critical period in the whole of
my swotting career, the hard work wasn't working!

"Give it a rest, Cath," said Dad. "Relax!"

"Fresh air and exercise," said Mum. "Compulsory
prescription!"

So, one February afternoon, when the light that had

never dawned was already fading, I called Captain, Irish lurcher and my very own — my only — faithful follower, and set off to walk up to the moor.

The blisteringly cold wind tore at my hair and a fine rain was stinging my scalp like a high-powered shower. Offering thanks to the unknown parishioner who'd donated his anorak to the jumble — and thence to Dad — I zipped it up to my throat, and followed Captain up the hill. Bad weather never stopped him; he tore off through the wind like some medieval hunting hound.

The moor was wind-swept, treeless and dark with brittle brown heather under a leaden sky, a Brontë-land film set that matched my mood. Apart from my burning ambition for city life, I have a lot in common with the Brontës: daughter of the vicarage, plain as Charlotte, shy as Anne, tall as Emily. I've even got Branwell's untamed mop of dark brown hair!

I strode up the track thinking about those Brontë women. Even if you never read the books you can't miss them in these parts; they used to live just across the hills and now they're all around us: Brontë biscuits, Brontë garage, Brontë hairdressing salon. A bit of a laugh, that last one, when the sisters obviously never had their hair done in their lives. Well, they had a hard life, those girls — but at least they never had to learn chemistry, I reflected, as I scrambled to the top of the ridge, and paused to catch my breath.

I gazed across the dark, dead moorland, my mind teetering between A-level chemistry and the Brontë industry — nice little earners, both: the chemistry guaranteed my future career, the Brontë Tea Shoppe, my holiday job. And over to the west, signposted by the rain clouds streaming over it, lay the city — my goal. I suddenly had the urge to get back to work. Maybe I'd be more successful now I'd had a break.

"Captain! Captain! here, boy..." The dratted dog was nowhere in sight. I put my fingers between my teeth and blew a shrill whistle, loud enough to cut through the wind. The air was rent with answering shrieks. I had a split-second vision of hags and witches tearing across the moor, and froze, inside now, as well as out. I shut my eyes and thought of those old folk tales on Dad's bookshelves — of boggarts and bogles and hobgoblins. It was easy to believe in foul fiends up there on the black clouded moor. But a deep, angry, human voice brought me back to my senses.

"What the hell...?"

And I heard Captain bark, not his usual deep, friendly bark, but a high-pitched, nervous tone. Something had upset him. I ran down the dip in the sheep track, round the bend, and came on a scene from one of those old black-and-white films I watch on wet-and-windy afternoons. Captain lay on his side, eyes closed, mouth bloodied, whimpering. A horse stood close by, great shudders passing down its flanks. And across the track, on a bank of old heather, sat a man, clutching his shoulder and moaning, his face white with pain.

Of course, I knew just what to do. Ignoring both horse and rider, I rushed over to my dog. After all, Captain's my best friend.

"Oh, Captain, love, what's happened to you?" He moaned a little and put out his tongue to lick my hand. I watched, horrified, as blood oozed from a gash in his black lips.

"What has it done to you?" I glared up at the horse. It rolled its great eyes and snickered at me, revealing huge yellow teeth, and my courage faded. I buried my head in Captain's rough coat and hugged him to me.

"The dog... it startled her..." the man gasped.

I turned to face him, furious, ready to defend my precious hound against his vicious animal. But as soon as I looked at him, the words were stopped in my mouth. Wild black hair spilled out of his riding hat over the collar of his Barbour jacket; grey eyes glowered from a dark, unshaven face, the wide mouth drawn thin with pain. My God! I thought, it's Heathcliff!

I stared at the Heathcliff-man and gasped for breath as if it was me who'd just been thrown from the horse. My stomach churned, my mouth dried. I swallowed hard and tried to speak.

"Are you hurt?" I squeaked.

He nodded, then winced. "Bloody shoulder," he said; it didn't sound like cursing in his posh, southern voice. "If you could bring my horse over," he went on, "I could pull myself back up."

I almost laughed aloud at the idea of me leading a horse. In spite of my country childhood — perhaps even because of it — I was terrified of the creatures. So terrified that I found the courage to go over and face the man himself.

"Let me help you up," I said.

He stared up at me, doubtfully at first, then as he took in my height and my broad, strong hands, he made a move forwards, but groaning, sank back again. He looked so pale and ill that I forgot to be shy, awkward, embarrassed.

"Hang on!" I scrabbled in Dad's jacket pockets. They're usually lined with odd notes, bits of string, ancient handkerchiefs — with any luck there might be a scarf. Finally I produced a black clerical scarf — left there since Dad last took a funeral, no doubt. The very thing — unless you were superstitious.

"Here — this'll do." I leaned over and slipped the scarf round his neck.

I've done Mum's village-hall first-aid course four times now; it used to be her attempt to find friends for me. It never made me any friends but it did wonders for my biology grades. I twisted the scarf into a 'collar and cuff' sling, and without giving myself time to feel embarrassed, sat down beside him and gently took his hand.

"Just one little movement, then you can rest it," I told him.

He flinched as I lifted his arm and placed it carefully in the sling. When I had finished he sighed deeply, closed his eyes, and rested for a moment against me. And against my five winter layers of Damart vest, cotton polo, brushed check lumber shirt, Aran sweater and borrowed anorak. But even through that lot I could feel the pressure of his head on my shoulder. I looked down into his dark, tortured face and a surge of weakness engulfed me, as if I, too, were injured. Which, in a way, I was.

For a moment, we sat close in the heather, his head against my shoulder, my arm supporting him. Like a courting couple in reverse, I reflected. I always get the supporting role, comes of being so tall, I suppose. But I didn't mind just then, I could have gone on supporting him forever!

He turned his head and smiled up at me. His eyes were the cool grey of a summer dawn, the lashes blacker than any mascara.

"A beautiful stranger out here in the wilds," he murmured. "Are you real?"

Beautiful, he'd called me! Sodden hair, reddened nose and the usual spot on my chin — but beautiful all the same. The word flowed through me and I stood up.

"Oh, aye, I'm real enough," I said, wincing at the Yorkshire in my voice. "Shall you be able to walk?"

"I think so, if you could just help me to stand..." He put his free hand down and pushed himself off the heather bank. I leant over to help him up.

"Aaahh!" he exclaimed, and grasped my arm so hard I almost over-balanced and sank down with him into the heather again. But my long, strong feet held firm and I steadied us both. Then, taking a deep breath, he drew himself upright. For a moment he stood looking down at me. Glory be! — six feet two, at the very least. I grinned shakily up at him.

"Well, you obviously have the knack," he said. Oh, if that had been true, I'd have had a boyfriend or three by then. But, swotty, churchy, flat-chested and nearly six feet tall, I'd yet to meet the lad who wasn't put off. As I looked up at this stranger, who'd just called me beautiful, I felt almost fragile, feminine. Not helpless, however.

"I'll help you down to the village," I announced.

"What about your dog?"

We both glanced at Captain, who was already sitting up, shaking his head from side to side and scratching his ear.

"He was probably only stunned," I said, knowing just how he felt. "He'll follow us."

The man stared hard at Captain, as if checking him over. Probably had dogs of his own and knew what to look for.

"Only cut his lip, I think, he said. "It'll be a bit sore, though, won't it boy?"

Captain, detecting sympathy, slunk across, whined sadly and settled himself on the stranger's boots. I don't blame him — could have done the same. We stood together, looking fondly down at the dog, saying nothing. And I knew I was lost.

Anyone who loves my dog...

"You know, if you could just bring Poll over here and help me to mount, I'll ride back and save you a lot of trouble," he said.

I didn't want to be saved any trouble; I'd carry him down the track myself, if necessary. I glared at the horse, envying her task; she'd carry him off to wherever they'd come from and out of my life forever. The thought made me take a desperate decision.

"The jogging about might harm your shoulder." I spoke with my mother's authority. "I'll lead the horse and walk you down to the village."

I couldn't believe this was me — so decisive, so confident and offering to lead a horse!

Unaware of this revolution, he called the horse over and handed me the reins. I took them without daring to glance at the huge animal behind me and we set off, in a strange sort of procession, down the fell-side. The tall young man grasped my arm and leaned close to me; Captain, quite recovered and apparently as attracted as I was, trotted at his heels. The horse, thank heaven, kept her distance.

With the wind now at our backs, we made good progress down to the village. A pity, I could have gone on to the next town — to the city — to the ends of the earth! But Thorneywood is only a mile down the fell and we soon arrived at the church gates. That's where he stopped.

"Thanks, I'll be all right now," he said.

He was looking towards the high iron gates of The Old Vicarage. Not the working vicarage, my home, a bland, modern, brick building down the village, but the seventeenth-century, stone-built, gables, mullioned Old Vicarage, sold for a six-figure fortune to some wealthy bloke from down South. Like the man who stood beside me, perhaps?

"Is this where you live?" I asked.

"Came yesterday," he answered briefly, breathing with difficulty. He turned to lead the horse up to the iron gates and winced as he moved away. "Thanks for all your help," he said.

My mind whirled: I could hear the clang of the gates, see him disappearing up the gravelled drive. Anyone who could afford to live up at The Old Vicarage would not be socialising with the likes of me!

"Wait!" I called. He stopped in front of the gates. "Er — you ought to see a doctor," I said rapidly. "You may have bruised ribs as well as a dislocated shoulder."

"So, you're not just my beautiful rescuer, then?" he asked, smiling painfully. "You're a nurse?"

"No, I'm not," I admitted. "But my mother is." A brilliant idea flooded through my reeling brain. "She'll be home now," I said. "She'll make you comfortable and then ring Accident and Emergency down in Halifax, save you waiting around at hospital."

He hesitated. I held my breath. Had I been too bossy? Frightened him off? But he just nodded his shaggy head in the direction of The Old Vicarage.

"They're all out," he said. I wondered briefly who he meant by 'all'. Parents? Family? Wife? I pushed the thought away.

"Well, surgery's over, the Clinic's closed — you'd better come and see Mum."

"If you're quite sure she won't mind..."

"Oh no, she always helps out in emergencies," I lied, suddenly generous with Mum's hard-earned free time.

"What about Poll?" He glanced at the horse.

"Oh, I'll come back and take care of her," I said, grandly, sweeping away years of horse-avoidance and a total ignorance of stable manners. I tied the reins to the iron railings, even going so far as to plant a vague slap on the creature's neck, in what I hoped was a professional manner. Then I took the rider's hand once more and led him down the village street, past the church, up the lane and home to the real vicarage.

Mum replaced the funeral scarf with a pink foam collar-and-cuff sling. Then she cleaned him up and led him out to her car before we could even exchange a word! I stood on our drive, watching him fold himself into her little car. Mum fixed his safety-belt, closed his door, then shot off back into the house for her bag.

He looked steadily at me, as if willing me forwards, then he smiled and said something I couldn't hear. I was just moving closer, when Mum came racing back, threw herself into the car — and they were gone!

And all I knew about him was his name: Edward Lindsay, not Heathcliff. I mooched back into the house, haunted by the thought that he'd called me to the car window and I'd never replied. I could see the shape of his lips, his tongue against his teeth. Cathy! — that was it, that was what he was saying! He'd called my name and I'd missed the chance to go to him. Hell and damnation, what a great daft lump I was! To prove it, I stumped upstairs and gave myself a chemistry revision test. I failed.

It was Dad who went down to see to Poll. He reported that the stables were warmer than our house and there was another horse to keep Poll company.

"Expensive horses," he said. "Seriously rich, our newcomers."

Horsy and wealthy — and a family, installed at the most beautiful house in the village — just the sort of guy to go for me! Gloomily, I tended to Captain's lip, gave him a very mushy supper, and let him sleep on my bed — though whether for his comfort or my own, I wasn't quite sure. I flopped down beside him and opened my chemistry text book. But I didn't learn a thing.

As soon as I heard Mum's car pull in, I abandoned chemistry and dashed downstairs. But my ex-Heathcliff wasn't there.

"Badly bruised, not dislocated," Mum explained. "I've taken him home. Oh, and he said to tell you thanks for rescuing him," she added. "Sensible girl!"

"Yeah, aren't I just?" I said, bitterly. It was all so different in books.

After supper, I pretended to revise and after that, to sleep. I heard Mum come upstairs, hesitate outside my room, then, seeing the light was out, move on. With relief, I turned to pull back my curtains. the wind was up again, shifting clouds across the moon, shadows over the moor and over my mind. 'Beautiful,' he'd called me. But I wasn't. Was I?

I peered at my reflection in the long window. My baggy tee-shirt hung loose from my square shoulders, like a fluorescent shift; my long arms looked almost shapely rather than thin, and dark, as if tanned. Yeah, well, anybody looks beautiful in moonlight. I picked up a handful of tangled hair and pulled it up on top of my head. Perhaps I should wear it like that next time...

What next time? What if I never met him again? Of course he knew where I lived, even knew my name, but he was a wealthy incomer. Up on the moor he'd looked so boyish, but his face was weathered and stubbly — could be twenty-something, old enough to marry, especially when you're rich. And I was seventeen and poor — the arithmetic was irrelevant. He might have a family — children, as well as horses! I reached out and grasped my chemistry book, clutching it to me, as if to ward off the worst of my fears.

Captain woke me at first light, and suddenly I knew what I had to do. Pulling jeans and sweater on top of my night-shirt, I took the surprised animal out for his first run of the day. Down the lane, across the graveyard and out alongside the big wrought-iron gates of The Old Vicarage. The porch light was on — and a light on the ground floor, in the far corner of the house. Was that his? Perhaps he'd slept downstairs so's not to disturb — who? I leaned on the heavy gate, peering in through the iron curlicues at the lighted window, willing it to open. But of course it didn't.

The door did, though. I saw a figure in the lighted porch, standing quite still, apparently staring at me. I pulled Captain back into the shadow. He gave a little yelp of protest and the figure leaned forward a little, as if to listen: small, blonde, wrapped in a heavy velvety robe, undoubtedly female and tousled-looking as if she had just got out of bed...

Through tears, I saw her pick up a couple of bottles of milk and go back inside. To tend to him, no doubt. To take care of her — what? What was he to her? Her son, perhaps, I told myself hopefully. But I didn't really believe it; even in the gloomy morning light I could see she wasn't old enough. Sadly, I led Captain back across the graveyard, envying its peaceful inhabitants.

Later that day, a bouquet! We never send flowers in our family, flowers being the cause of more dissent in church than the appointment of women bishops: who should do the altar, who could manage January, and the fuss about Harvest, Easter, Christmas! Dad greeted my bouquet with suspicion.

"Don't worry, they're not going into church," I assured him, slipping the card into my jeans pocket. I read it later, on my own, in the quiet of the kitchen.

Dear Cathy,

Many thanks for rescuing me — and for taking care of
Poll. I hope Captain's mouth isn't too painful and I do
hope you'll find time to come and see me — very soon.
Edward Lindsay

I read it, re-read it, read it again. It fluttered in my
trembling hand. My face was burning, my heart really
did go pit-a-pat. I felt as if I'd float to the ceiling. So it's
true — all that stuff I'd read about in books, listened to
in songs, laughed to scorn in Mum's magazines — it's
all true!

Of course, I hadn't forgotten the woman on the
porch. Perhaps she's just a servant, I thought,
conveniently forgetting the velvet dressing-gown. A
family like that would have a housekeeper. Or a nanny...

Groaning almost with pain, I raced upstairs, flung
myself on my bed and sank into a deep, dark gloom. At
lunch-time I emerged to toast a sandwich for Dad and
play with a bit of salad myself, and as soon as it was
decently 'visiting hours', I set off to The Old Vicarage.

The woman who opened the door was the one who'd
been on the porch earlier. Prettier, close-up, and much,
much too young to be his mother. And you'd have to be
mad to employ such a dishy blonde as a housekeeper/
nanny.

"Yes?" she asked.

"I... er... I er... came to see how Edward is," I muttered.

"Oh, you must be the girl who rescued him
yesterday," she laughed; a sweet, quiet laugh. "Well, I
think he's sleeping just now, but do come in."

Her voice sounded posh, southern, a lighter version of
his. I followed her into a long stone-flagged hall, still
piled with open packing cases.

"So sorry about the mess — I just haven't had the

time, with Ted's accident — you know how it is..." Her accent told of an expensive education, her petite figure slotted into tiny, velvety leggings and a vast angora designer-sweater. Neat as a kitten, she picked her way between mounds of cushions, piles of books and stacks of china. I'd never hated anyone — never cared enough to bother — until then. She disappeared ahead of me into a room at the far end of the hall. I heard voices: hers clear and confident, his drowsy, complaining.

"That girl," I heard her say; and then, soothingly, "All right, darling, I'll tell her..."

I turned back in panic — she was going to get rid of me! I should never have come, never have taken him up on the invitation. People of their sort, they were always issuing vague invitations that had no meaning. And the flowers were merely a charming formality — probably sent by her, his wife. As I admitted the possibility, tears welled up. Frantically, I searched for an escape route but I knew I'd never make it back across the cluttered hall without breaking something. Tall and clumsy, that was me — yes, and daft with it! How could he have thought me beautiful? How could I have hoped he'd be free?

She came towards me, small, dainty, neat, slim, beautiful, graceful, fair... the adjectives came crowding. And older, I saw now, thirty-something, perhaps. But even so, the right age for him. As she put up her hand to tuck in a strand of hair, I saw she was wearing a wedding ring.

"Just go on in, he's awake now." She smiled up at me; knowing I was no rival.

I nodded curtly and picked my way over to the room at the end of the hall.

"Come in." His voice was stronger now, deeper, more masculine than it had been the previous day. "Oh,

Cathy, I'm so glad you came..."

He looked glad — really, he did. He was propped on pillows on a sort of day-bed in what would obviously be a study when the bookshelves were filled. He patted the end of his bed and, in a daze, I went over and perched there.

We didn't say anything for a while. He looked at me and I wished I'd washed my hair, bleached it blonde, had it fashionably cropped as Mum wanted me to. I looked at him and wished I didn't blush so pink, so often.

"So how's Captain now?" he asked, eventually.

"What?" I asked, as if I'd never heard of my ever-faithful friend.

"His mouth," he prompted. "Is it healing?"

"Oh, er, yes, yes, it is..." My sparkling repartee faded under his gaze.

"He's eating all right?" He sounded really concerned.

I took a deep breath and tried to concentrate. "Well, he has to chew on one side," I said, "so I gave him slops for dinner today."

Oh, great, Cath Longshaw, just the sort of cultured, sophisticated conversation he's used to, no doubt.

"Poor lad," Edward smiled fondly — at me or the thought of Captain? "I'm afraid Poll caught him with her hoof. She wouldn't have hurt him purposely — she's too gentle."

I nodded, as I knew all about gentle horses.

"Well, you must have noticed that, when you stabled her last night," he went on. "It was good of you to take over like that..." He beamed admiration at me.

What could I say?

"Well, actually..." and I confessed all. I told him how Dad had stabled Poll, because I was afraid of her — of all horses.

"But you led her off the moor," he said.

"Yeah, well, there was nothing else for it, was there?" I blustered. I could hardly admit I did it just because... because what? "That was different."

He smiled and suddenly looked younger, maybe just on twenty rather than twenty-something. So I smiled back.

"So, how are you feeling now?" he asked, rather briskly.

"That's my line," I said, and wished I hadn't. What if it sounded too sharp, too knowing, too whatever-it-was-I-did-wrong whenever I was with a boy?

But he just laughed. "You're right," he said. "But that's typical."

"Typical."

"Of us."

Us! He put us together?

"We're all opposite, you and I, aren't we?" he went on. "You know — knight in shining armour rescuing fair maiden?" He put out a hand to me. Was it a gesture or an offer? "You're my fair maiden in shiny anorak who came to the rescue of the dark rider in distress. Like a legend inside-out."

Ah, but what about the other fair maiden outside the door? And as if I'd conjured it up, there came an irritated exclamation from the hallway.

"Hell and damnation..."

"That's Caro, sorting out the rest of her crates. She's determined to get them finished before her husband arrives."

"Her husband?" I almost choked.

"Yes, my dear brother-in-law — always working too hard to be any use at home," he smiled. "So I came over with the horses and now I'm no use either, poor Caro."

I couldn't answer, just sat there, bedazzled, bemused,

as he talked about his veterinary degree course in Liverpool, his sister Caro and her computer-wizard husband.

"Oh — I haven't even asked if you'd like some tea — shall I call Caro?"

I breathed deeply, shakily, and shook my head. I wanted nothing more than to be alone with him. But I couldn't tell him that, could I?

"Well, it's nice enough with just us two." His voice was soft and breathy now — or was that just because of his bruised ribs?

I nodded — not too eagerly, I hoped.

"It was all my fault," Edward went on. "I should never have taken Poll up there so soon after her long journey. Travelling always upsets her."

He spoke so tenderly about the horse I was almost jealous. But then he reached out a hand again, this time looking straight at me.

"No hard feelings?"

Hard feelings? Oh no, all my feelings were melting soft just then.

"No hard feelings," I whispered. And, suddenly daring, I gripped his finger-tips. We sat for — how long? Touching fingers, holding hands, looking long and deep into each other's eyes. His were pale, grey-to-green in that light, with those long black lashes no man should own. And mine would be their usual ordinary hazel, with stubby lashes to match my brown, frizzy hair. Well, at least I'd got it piled on my head, and at least my face was clear and nearly spot-free today. But he didn't look at my face or my hands or my too-square shoulders, my long, thin arms. Just into my eyes. And I gazed into his...

Soon be spring, now; the slopes of the Pennines show a

hint of green haze, though the tops are white with snow. In the churchyard clumps of snowdrops lift up their little white heads, and daffodils thrust their green spears higher by the day. The winds still tear across the moor but now they rip the ragged clouds and the sun streams out. Green and gold and blue and shining — spring surges through me. I'm filled with energy, excitement, anticipation! Edward will be back at Easter.

The Blue Madonna
Linda Kempton

October 14th 1914

The house is different now. From the moment I first brought my child back here I knew that it had changed. My aunt waited to welcome me home, as I knew she would. I expected it; took it for granted. What I hadn't expected was that others would be waiting too; almost imperceptibly at first, but each day growing clearer, stronger. It is William, my child, who has brought them here. Until his arrival, they were silent. Now I feel them gathering.

I have not spoken to my aunt about this. Or to Zillah, who looks at me darkly as she hobbles about the kitchen. I sometimes catch her muttered prayers for my soul and sometimes, inexplicably, she calls me Rachael. I am Anna, I tell her, Anna.

Since my mother's death my aunt has protected me; made allowances. According to her, my being with child at sixteen can be explained by the loss of my mother: in the midst of life we are in death, although life, in its turn, can rend death's veil. Thus William is allowed, perhaps even accepted as symbolic of the triumph of life. Perhaps. Only if William's father returns from this awful war, will I fully believe it.

So I am protected. I am delicate, vulnerable. I am fortunate, too. Other girls in my position have been removed from society, their sanity questioned. I must take care. I must not say too much.

I spend a lot of my time in the kitchen. My aunt is motherly and I need her warmth. The sound of the beating of eggs, the sight of bread dough rising by the fire, the kittens, curled beside the range, the sound of William's suckling in the midst of all this; these things, and my aunt, keep me safe. Zillah, my old nurse, disapproves, silently.

I try to tell my aunt how the house has changed, how I sense things which should not be there, how these things sense me. Perhaps I should not have spoken. I risk a great deal; I cannot afford to have my sanity questioned, although at times I question it myself.

Zillah looks at me, her head on one side in that peculiar, bird-like way of hers, and talks of the past repeating itself. She has been here for many years, was the servant of the people who lived here before us; indeed, was in service here at a younger age than I am now. It seems the house has witnessed a story similar to my own. She wonders why I am not more ashamed, as if I should parade my shame for her satisfaction. Oh, Zillah, if only you knew.

She shifts her old bones in the creaking Windsor chair, sips from her tea-cup, and, her disapproval forgotten for a while, begins to tell me the story of this house and its people, when another war raged and Florence Nightingale held her lamp high in the field hospitals.

Rachael looked up at the huge Georgian house. Trees loomed darkly over the red brick walls, and chimneys disappeared into a tangle of greenery. Even in daylight the house looked dark.

The sound of the carriage which had brought her home grew fainter. She felt she had been away for a long, long time. The baby stirred in her arms and she bent her mouth to his ear. "This is where you live," she told him.

She held her cheek against his. He was worth

everything: the gossip, the sidelong glances, the disapproval worn like a second skin; even having to leave home for those endless months. She was fortunate to return.

She looked up at the house again. There was something not quite right about it, something she couldn't quite place. She turned her head, feeling herself observed. Aunt Bea was in the dining room, looking out at her from the big, square-paned window. A solitary magpie screeched from the yew tree. Aunt Bea lifted a hand in greeting.

Rachael heard footsteps clacking across the wooden hallway and was suddenly shot through with a fierce longing for her mother.

The brass lion knocker thudded as the door swung open. Aunt Bea stood in the dark hallway, tall and reed-thin, her face in shadow. And Rachael, remembering, was five years old again. "Say hello to Great Aunt Bea," her mother had said. But she couldn't speak, couldn't say a word to this woman who loomed immense and witch-like, her mouth a vivid red gash.

Now Rachael had the impression of a smile, of eyes flashing in the cool shadows. She held the baby close. "Where is my mother?"

Aunt Bea didn't answer. The silence expanded.

"Have you been to church?" she asked.

"To church?"

"A woman newly delivered of child must not enter a house until she has entered a church. Surely you know that?"

Rachael frowned. She tried to look into the woman's face. But Aunt Bea stood too far back in the dark hall; her face was indistinct. Then she stepped forward, hunching her shoulders into a coat.

Rachael ran up the steps, her long skirt in one hand,

the baby clutched against her breast. "I want to see my mother first. I have to."

Aunt Bea took hold of Rachael's arm. "It must be done immediately."

"Please, Aunt Bea. Please."

"You must come at once." Aunt Bea banged the door shut. She dug a bony hand into the small of Rachael's back, propelled her down the steps. "You have only to enter the church," she said as they walked along. "Nothing else is necessary for the time being. You need not see the vicar."

But the vicar was there when they arrived. Rachael stood with her sleeping child beside the altar rail, while Aunt Bea hovered in the ancient porch. The vicar, emerging from the vestry, looked up and saw Rachael standing there. His face paled. He turned so quickly that he almost tripped. The slam of the vestry door woke the sleeping child and Rachael shivered as she pulled him close. Her feet clanged on the metal grille as she hurried back down the aisle. She stifled a sob. This was how it would be from now on. Even Zillah, her beloved nurse, would not look her in the face. Even the vicar, the man of God, had turned from her. Did that mean God had turned his face too?

A shaft of sunlight lit a window to Rachael's left. She looked up to see a gleaming blue Madonna with her child, white as lily flowers. God had smiled His favour on this young mother; surely He wouldn't turn His face from her.

Comforted, she walked home silently.

Back home, the vast, wood-panelled hall seemed like an old friend. Her eyes scanned upwards, along the three sides of the galleried landing, and then down into the hall again: the barometer on the wall, the oak chest with its enormous bowl of shiny green leaves and rusty chrysanthemums. An old hall in an old house. Polished and warm. Safe.

Later, they sat in the kitchen drinking tea. It was warm and tidier than Rachael was used to, now that Aunt Bea was living there. There was no sign of Zillah's constant pile of mending and teetering piles of books, borrowed from Father's library; the kitchen had been invaded by order. Even the click of the grandfather clock seemed tidier.

"Where's Zillah?"

"She has the afternoon off. Her friend is ill and in want of comfort." Aunt Bea sat at the far end of the table, like a black shadow, not moving except to pour the tea and pass sandwiches. She watched Rachael silently.

"Have some more tea," she whispered, until Rachael felt they might float away on a tannin tide. She felt floaty. Unreal.

"Where is my mother?"

Tears pulled at Rachael's eyes. She stared hard at the floor so that she wouldn't blink and shed them.

"My poor girl." Aunt Bea scraped back her chair and moved round the table towards her. She laid her hand over Rachael's and next to the baby's. "Such young skin," the woman crooned, "so smooth."

Rachael saw the hands through her tears: Aunt Bea's, wrinkled and paper-dry; her own, smooth and unlined; the baby's, translucent, his nails like shiny pink shells on a beach. And then the hands seemed to shimmer and merge; they became unreliable. Youth and age were alike, meant nothing.

"I want my mother. Please tell me where she is."

"Rachael, I'm very concerned about you, my dear."

Rachael closed her eyes and willed herself to be calm. "Please tell me, Aunt Bea."

143

The woman rose and began to stack the cups and plates from the table. Then she stood with her back to the fireplace and clasped her hands in front of her in a prim little gesture.

"You are a very foolish girl, Rachael Hamilton. You will not accept what has happened to you; what has happened to all of us. Your mother would have been so unhappy. Poor Martha."

Aunt Bea's face was in shadow, the features blurred. Rachael could see only the red mouth moving. She threw her head back with a sigh. She stared at the wooden clothes pulley suspended from the high ceiling, as if she had never seen it before, as if the regimented tea-towels might suddenly speak. Her head began to swim and the tea-towels fluttered; they lifted and danced as if by some invisible breeze.

"Your mother," said Aunt Bea, "my dear niece, Martha..." and instantly Rachael's eyes were on her face once more. No sound came from the moving mouth. Rachael studied the foolish contortions of the old woman's lips. She stared at the clasped hands, at the folds of skin hanging loose round her great-aunt's neck, then at her mouth again.

"...you've been through a great deal, recently, my dear. Death and birth. Everyone finds it a shock, at first."

Rachael rubbed her hands across her eyes. She was terribly tired. Aunt Bea's face floated in front of her, swam in and out of focus. She was so tired.

Later, she lay in her own bed with her back against the pillows, the baby's cheek against her breast, his fingers splayed out against her skin. His eyes searched her as he sucked. The rhythmic tugging on her nipple gave her such peace, such love for the child. She was keeping him alive with her own body. Whatever happened from now on, she would have her son. "My son." She said it out loud and smiled at the ripple of pleasure the words set up in her.

She settled him in his cradle. There was a connecting door between his room and hers. She left it open so that she could hear him when he cried, and so that she could see the soft glow of the night-light through the empty rectangle, picking out shapes, comforting. Aunt Bea would want her to blow it out but she would not.

Rachael was just getting back into bed when she heard the sound of carriage wheels on the drive. The reflection of its lamps passed along the drawn curtains. She ran to the window.

"Mother."

She lifted the curtain but the carriage pulled away, disappeared from sight. Only someone using the drive to turn. She let the curtain fall and walked slowly back to bed again.

"It wasn't your grandmother, after all," she whispered through the open door.

Her head was hot against the pillow. She lay on her back, exhausted but sleepless. She felt so alone.

"Mother," she whispered. "Why aren't you here?"

She heard the clock strike midnight.

October 20th 1914
Sometimes I have the strangest sensation that when I put William in his cradle, it is already occupied. I hear cries in the night and they are so full of anguish that I wake with my heart almost breaking for my baby's pain. But they are not his cries. He lies sleeping, not woken by echoes, as I am. I should feel afraid but I do not. I feel a yearning ache which almost suffocates me; which bears me down with the weight of its sorrow.

When William does cry, I am not always the first to his

side. But she flits out of sight when I enter the room. She is an impression only, a glimpse caught at the corner of the eye: long dark hair, a white night-dress. I am the intruder, not she.

I tell Zillah and I see the flicker of fear on her face. She does not share these sensations or witness what I have seen and heard and felt. She does not need to; she once knew in the flesh what I merely glimpse in the spirit. She knows that I am not mad. But she is afraid. I wish she would tell me more.

Rachael woke suddenly. Her eyes stared wide in the blackness. Something was wrong. The night seemed brittle; as though it might snap in two at the click of her fingers. Her heart banged against her chest. Blackness. Only blackness. The door to the baby's room was closed.

She threw back the bedclothes. Edging her way to the door, she groped for the handle. The dim light washed over her as the door swung open. She could see the little mound of clothes in the baby's cot. He was safe.

But no, he was not safe. The cot was empty. Her baby was gone.

She ran to the other door and banged on it with fear. Banged it and banged it with the flat of her hand. Then pulled it open onto the night-time landing. Light from the little room spilled onto the wall and floor. Her eyes travelled the gallery, searching.

Then a pencil of light from the farthest corner. She clutched at the banister rail, felt her way along towards the light. She pushed the door so hard that it banged against the dressing table behind it.

"Hello, Rachael."

Aunt Bea held the baby in the crook of her arm. She was feeding him. She was feeding him with a bottle: a glass, banana-shaped bottle. The woman pulled it from his mouth and Rachael saw the leathery teat, old and mis-shapen like a hag's brown nipple. Aunt Bea sat the baby up to wind him. He was bound tightly in swaddling clothes, bandaged like an Egyptian mummy.

Rachael wanted to scream but she said, quietly, "Give him to me. Give him to me or I'll kill you. He's mine."

"Poor Rachael. Of course he's yours, my dear. But when you fail to wake to his screaming then someone else must look to his welfare. If you are not able."

She couldn't speak. She clutched at the side of her night-gown, her fingers opening and closing on the cool cotton. She tried to control the sound of her breathing, tried to appear calm.

"He wasn't screaming. I'd have heard."

"It's not given to every woman to be a mother. You must not count yourself a failure on that score. And of course you are really only a child yourself. Only sixteen."

The light from the candle beside the bed flickered on Aunt Bea's face, yet Rachael could see nothing except the glitter of eyes and a smile that seemed to live independently.

"Please give him to me."

"Of course."

Rachael crossed the room to the side of the bed. Aunt Bea did not hold the child out to her, so she had to lean forward and pull him from the woman's arms. His skin was pallid and tiny beads of sweat stood out across his brow. Milk trickled from the corner of his mouth.

"You shouldn't have done that. He won't feed from me if you give him a bottle."

"Better the bottle than a wet-nurse, surely?" Aunt Bea glittered in the candlelight.

Rachael turned and walked from the bed, her hand trembling beneath the baby's head.

Without warning, she was plunged into darkness. In the sudden dark she banged her head against the open door. The pain and the shock smashed her careful control. She began to shake, to cry. She held the baby tight. She might drop him. There was silence apart from the sound of her own breathing, rasping against the tightness of her throat.

"How clumsy of me, my dear. How careless of me to knock the candle."

Rachael ran across the landing and bolted her bedroom door. "Help me," she whispered.

November 8th 1914

It is not merely the girl and the baby who inhabit this house with us. There is someone else: a darker presence; the sharp corner of the triangle. When she leans over William's cradle, it is not with love but with a lust for possession.

Sometimes when I lift him, I can feel her at my shoulder, and I know that if I turn around she will wrench the child from my arms. I hold him more tightly, cling to him so that she will not succeed. I wish I knew how to protect him. I wish my mother was here.

There are times when William lies in his cradle and a sudden smile flits across his face. He is following something with his eyes. He follows as far as he can and then turns his head so that he can see still further. The smile broadens and becomes a gurgle of laughter. At other times, I see him start; his eyes widen and he begins to cry, a high, fearful cry. I pick him up but he will not be soothed, for he knows, as I know, that she is still there. Sometimes I hear her breathing. I am afraid she might breathe me in.

I do not know who to turn to for help. I am no longer sure of my sanity. Zillah tells me their story in mean little parcels, when I crave it all.

Rachael laid the baby on her bed. She must dress quickly. Trying to work as fast as possible and caught between the desire for speed and the need for quiet, she pulled at the wardrobe doors. Anything would do.

But the wardrobe was empty. Her clothes were gone.

The drawers? But no, they were empty too.

She rushed to the chair and began to put on yesterday's clothes. Her fingers shook, buttons refused to fasten, she couldn't find her shoes. But they were there, kicked beneath the bed. She slipped them on. She wrapped Michael in his shawl and tiptoed to the door.

But no. Better wait till Aunt Bea was asleep again.

She wasn't asleep now. The landing creaked. She could hear her coming nearer; slowly, slowly, the footsteps reached the door. Then stopped. Rachael listened, her ear pressed against the wooden panels. She could hear the woman listening too; she could hear her breathing. Then movement. Slowly the footsteps receded, slowly the creaking grew fainter. She heard the door close gently.

She had waited an hour. She was cold. She must go now.

Moonlight streamed through the panels at the side of the front door; it washed the hall with silver. A stained-glass cherub with fat cheeks stared down at her.

The door was always bolted and chained and locked. It was difficult to reach the top bolt while she was holding the baby. She tucked him in the crook of one arm and stood on tiptoe. Slowly, the bolt eased back.

The bottom one was easier and the chain slid free without a sound. She could almost breathe again. Only the lock now. She reached for the key. It was gone.

Fingers tapped at her spine. She turned quickly. The empty hall was quiet. No one stood in the shadows. She dropped down and patted one hand frantically over the doormat. But the key was not there.

Yes, yes it was: panic had made her careless. Now her fingers closed over it greedily. She stood quickly, too quickly. Coiled springs of dizziness circled her head. She leaned against the door until the feeling had passed.

Her fingers shook. The key would not go in straight. "Please," she whispered. "Please."

The baby stirred. The key turned.

She was out. Free in the night air. Free. She felt a rush of exhilaration, fear. Her feet padded down the long drive. The trees reached down towards her. Dark. Then she was out on the road, walking, walking fast. The village was deserted. Houses were curtained and blank. Only the moon shone.

The vicarage too was in darkness. But candlelight flickered through the pointed windows of the church, lighting up the Good Shepherd with His sheep. Rachael stepped through the avenue of yews; a soft breeze moved them, swayed them gently. The moon, riding high, silvered the gravestones and lit up a screaming gargoyle against the wall.

The oak door creaked as she pushed; groaned and protested so loudly, that she thought Aunt Bea might hear it. A single lamp hung at the front of the church. She could just pick out a figure halfway down the aisle, huddled against a pillar.

Aunt Bea glided towards her. "Hello, my dear," she said. "We hoped that you would come."

Another figure stepped out from the shadows. The vicar.

Rachael walked backwards as quickly as she could, down the aisle to the door. *No. No, leave me alone...* But the voice was only in her head. She dare not turn her back on them.

They were following, getting closer, hurrying, their eyes boring into her, running now, running. She pulled open the door and ran into the churchyard: round the back of the church, between gravestones, past tombs with metal railings, angels with marble wings, windows with jewelled saints. Rachael held her baby tight. She heard their footsteps behind her. Then the footsteps stopped and she found her own steps faltering. There were voices in the wind, calling her: the vicar's voice, Aunt Bea's. "She's here, Rachael. Come and look for yourself."

"You must look, my dear. Come and look. You must accept what God has seen fit to bring about."

Aunt Bea held out her hand. "My dear child, you must see for yourself. She is here."

The gravestone was below the painted window that had given her such comfort on her last visit; a blue Madonna and her child, white as lily flowers. Moonlight swept the lettering on the gravestone.

Martha Hamilton, Aged 39 Years
Widow of Joseph
Thy Will Be Done

Aunt Bea stepped out of the shadows. She held her hand out and Rachael took it. The vicar slipped silently away.

"You see, my dear. You see now. It is just the three of us. You, me, and our baby."

Michael stirred against his mother's breast and began to whimper quietly. Aunt Bea reached out and took him from Rachael. "Just the three of us, my dear. Just we three." She kissed the baby on his head and held him tight. "I shall carry him home. No need for you to exert yourself. No need at all."

December 7th 1914

It is ended. It was left to Zillah to call on the vicar and explain the changes in our house. Poor Zillah, hobbling and blinking like a pony up from the pit. I don't know how much longer she can continue.

My aunt has become strange. She tries to take William from me. I cannot do anything right with him as far as my aunt is concerned. I am a bad mother, it seems. But no, I am not. Only my aunt wishes to persuade me that I am, so that she might take control of my baby. I will not let her.

The vicar called on several occasions. He had to convince himself, and the bishop, it seems, that the house is haunted. Strange, I have avoided using that word till now.

The vicar performed the rite of exorcism with bell, book and candle. Now the house is quiet. I sit in the kitchen with Zillah and I am peaceful once more, now that they are gone.

I wish my aunt were so. She was strangely disturbed by the rite, and the vicar is a frequent visitor. I believe he prays with her.

William grows more beautiful each day. When he smiles, he smiles for me, or for Zillah who loves him like her own. She is my old nurse once more, all rancour forgotten now that she has become used to my situation and now that the house is free of those unwelcome presences. Yesterday, she took me to see the graves and we stood together, side by side, holding hands.

Martha Hamilton, Aged 39 Years
Widow of Joseph
Rachael, Their Daughter, Aged 16 Years
Thy Will Be Done

Beatrice Hamilton, Aged 72 Years
A Much Loved Aunt
Michael Hamilton, Dearest Nephew of Beatrice
Aged 21 Years

"She got him in the end," Zillah muttered. "Bea Hamilton always got what she wanted in the end." She squeezed my hand so hard I thought my knuckles would crack. As we walked back to the house, she told me about Rachael, whose situation was so like mine. Her lover was away, fighting in the Crimea, so there was no one to care when Aunt Bea locked her in her room and took charge of the child herself. Poor Rachael simply faded away and died.

I was haunted by Rachael, that much is certain; but she haunts me no longer. For my part, I shall stay hale and hearty and wait for my love to come back from the war. I shall haunt no one. As for my Aunt, only her sobs disturb the calm. I wish that I could help her.

Wakes
Caroline Pitcher

There she is!

She sits sideways on a white pony. She is still so small, so slight and brown-skinned and her eyes are blue-black as sloe-berries.

The pony's bells ring as it picks its way uphill through the market place, almost as steep in its incline as the moor she led me up last Summer. Me, and Thomas Tricklebank.

That day, the sun beat like a hammer.

I dressed my hair with *oile de bayes* and met with Will Gyte and George Lund. Off we set to find merriment at our village Wakes. There would be young women wanting money spent, and older women looking out for fine boys such as we.

"Hurry!" I hissed as we passed the ale-house, loud with fiddling and the low bassoon. I heard my father's voice too, thick with rum. It was a day to be out and about, not down my father's mine. This Wakes Day I would escape both him and Thomas Tricklebank.

Along the Holloway we went, dancing on the ruts, sniffing hungrily at the fat smell of swine roasting in Agnes Wood's yard. We pushed in through her gate but she shouted "Be off with you! He is not cooked through until mid-day."

We raced along Badger Lane and then the air began to shake. They were baiting a bull. He bellowed from his tethering by the churchyard. They taunted him and jabbed him with a sharpened stick. One man stuck him with a lead pick.

155

That was what began it all, the baiting of the beast.

He bellowed in rage and pain, and was answered by our own bull-calf, which was enclosed with the sheep in the pinfold.

I heard the splintering of the pinfold fence, and worse, "Samuel? *Samuel*!"

My father comes running out of the alehouse and through the village after us. No one else's father bothers about the pinfold. Just mine.

"Samuel!" His eyes are shot red. "Our beast is broken out from the pinfold and has taken the sheep with him. Go fetch them back at once! Here is Thomas come to help you."

My heart drops as Thomas Tricklebank trots towards us.

My father must provide for Thomas Tricklebank, because he is orphaned. Quarter Sessions gave him as an apprentice, to work our lead vein and our lands. Thomas's own father had set a fire to blast his lead ore and blasted apart himself instead. The mother had run off with a tinker, and many in the village sniggered, "What mother would not run from Thomas Tricklebank?"

"Dinna fret about your father's beast, Samuel," calls Thomas to me. "I have the small shoe for good luck."

He takes from his pocket a tiny shoe and waves it at us. It is one of a pair of fairy shoes. Some miners have them made by the cobbler in the next village. They take the shoes underground to please the fairies down there.

"The shoes didn't help *your* father, did they, Thomas!" sneers Will.

"Perhaps the fairy did not like that style!" cries George and throws his head back in a laugh. We laugh with him. It is not so funny, but that is our sport. That is how we are together.

Thomas puts the tiny shoe away and trots ahead of us. I see the back of his slight neck burned red by sun, right up to his jug-handle ears.

"We'll bring the sheep back first," I tell them.

We go through the underwood. Feathers float past us on the hot air. The fighting cocks screech and those who have put money on them roar encouragement.

"A cruel sport!" whispers Thomas, but only to me.

We discover the sheep eating hemp in Maria Bagshaw's garden and drive them back to the pinfold. While Thomas makes secure the fence, George shouts, "Away" and we three race up Maggot Lane and lie on a lush bank to rest. Will Gyte disappears. Soon he is back, passing round a flagon of his father's rhubarb wine.

Thomas comes panting up.

"Not you!" says Will, snatching away the flagon from Thomas's out-stretched hand.

So I drink Thomas's wine for him. It is thick and sweet. It gives me a thirst to rage all day and throw black spots before my eyes to make me sleep, but Thomas has not forgot what we should be doing.

"We still have your father's beast to find, Samuel," he says.

I groan, but he is right. I stand up. George and Will make no move to follow. Already George is puking up his rhubarb wine in the ditch. Will has seen skirts from over Ashbourne way. I want to go with him but I fear my father's anger if I do not bring back our beast.

"Come on then, Thomas Not-mucher," I say. "Let's find him."

"He will be cropping under some tree," says Thomas.

I put up my hand to shade my eyes. I see no beast, only endless lands and blue sky.

I wish I had not drunk that wine.

Up the moor-side we go, Thomas trotting, me

striding, for I will not fall behind him. The moor is pitted with mines and tussocks and is hard to walk. The hills around wear sparse trees like a coxcomb on their tops. There is little shade upon these hills.

Except on Ringinglow Rocks. That high hill is ridged with rocks that point like grey teeth from a gum. It is as if the earth has hurled them up towards the sky, but they would not go further and have stayed stuck there.

There is shade from thick elder trees, hawthorn, tall rosy willowherb and woodbine. There is roaring, too, as if a monster is imprisoned in the earth's bowels.

"He is up there!" squeaks Thomas, as if I were deaf.

We head up towards the roaring, past the mouth of Alice's Fortune, my father's new mine, named last week to the Barmaster. My father has given it my mother's name. Last summer, she died from her baby that would not be born. My father hopes that Alice's Fortune will make ours.

"Come on, Samuel!" shrills Thomas.

"Yes, come on, Samuel," echoes a pretty voice.

There she sits, sideways, high on a rock above the mine head, like a maid from the sea. Except that I can see her slight brown ankles below her skirt and her tiny, pink-nailed feet, and she holds a posy of flowers.

She smiles. Thomas grins back like the fool he is.

"So you have found your beast?" she says to him.

"It's *my* beast, not his," I say, and the growl in my voice is a surprise to me. "It belongs to my father, and so to me. It is not Thomas's beast at all. Thomas belongs to us. Thomas is *our* beast!"

She looks up at me. Her eyes are clouded blue-black as sloe-berries on a blackthorn branch. There is no white surround. I can hardly bear her gaze.

"So you must care for your beast, Samuel," she says, and slips down off the rock to walk with us. "Come on, then. Let us go fetch this beast home."

She skips ahead, her feet light on the rough ground, and we follow her.

The afternoon is cloudless. Far above is in the heavens sings a skylark. I blink in the sunlight and see the verdant growth that fills the earth's dips, like soft hair on a body. I see a harebell tremble on its stem, and the pale suns of scabious flowers. The world is so green and magical at this moment, it promises to last forever.

We head up the moor-side to Ringinglow Rocks.

There, in the shade of the overhanging stone, stands our beast. His head is down. He paws the ground and his small eyes are wild in his great head. This needs care. Bulls will kill from thirst in summer. Last night, beasts and sheep all called for water, but to my knowledge, no one paid heed. They were too busy drinking Pale Derby in the alehouse.

The girl turns. She is far below my shoulder. I see the round of her breasts push above her gown, golden-ripe as ripe acorns. Thomas looks at them too. If he were a dog, his pink tongue would be hanging to his chin.

She says, "Your beast is ill at ease. Do you think he sees spirits?"

I do not want to think of spirits. They say a traveller died up here some winters past. They say he was caught in a fierce blizzard and that he froze to death, stiff as an icicle. They say that in the next dale along, nine fine ladies danced to a fiddler and were turned to stone for impropriety. Their fiddler, too. And they talk about the Wirksworth Rider...

As if she knows my mind, the sloe-eyed girl says, "Perhaps your beast saw the Rider, forging up the moor from Wirksworth, with his head upon his saddle, and his line of pack ponies?"

Thomas's eyes are huge with fright.

"No ghosts dare ride over *our* moor!" I tell her. "Ghosts only show themselves to those who fear them. That is so, Thomas. Is it not?"

Thomas is trembling. I wonder if he shakes continually and I have not noticed before? But then he rallies, glances from one of us to the other, and runs at the beast to show bravery, flapping his arms like a young bird that cannot fly, crying, "Back you go! Back, beast!"

The beast snorts and turns. He runs not back down the moor-side, but pushes through a narrow gape into the rocks. We squeeze after him into dark that smells of rottenness.

His bulk looms just inside the cave.

"Don't startle him more, you milksop!" I hiss. "If he goes further, he may become stuck for ever. Much of my father's wealth is in his weight. Stay still!"

"No, I must return him to your father, Samuel!" cries Thomas, and again he runs at the beast, whose eyes roll in white rings, and whose nostrils froth like bubbled milk. His sides heave and he backs until he can go no further, until he is pressed against the cave wall.

With a roar like a river in full spate, the cave side falls. Earth showers down upon us, thick as hail. It fills my nose and mouth and eyes, and I fear it will have buried the girl and stopped her breath.

I claw snot and dust away. Earth still spins like ash around me. Stones and boulders roll across the cave floor, in an avalanche, for the beast has knocked down a cairn, but through the swirling earth I see her, standing still and quite possessed by calm.

And then a wail goes up.

"Skellingtons!" howls Thomas Tricklebank. "Dead skellingtons!"

High on a flat ledge, glimpsed through the spinning

dust, three skeletons sit side by side. Their backs are against a rock. Their knees are drawn up to their bony chins and their feet are thin and long.

I did not know that feet had so many bones.

One of the skeletons is small. It is a child, a grinning child.

"How long have they sat up there?" I ask.

"A long time indeed," says the girl.

Thomas wipes his hand across his clagged nose. He whimpers, "Dead... dead..." and rubs his sore eyes, and something stabs my chest. *Pity*.

I step forward and pat him on the shoulder. "There, there, Thomas," I say to comfort him. "Dinna weep, now."

The skeletons sit in their tomb, now open to the world. They grin.

"I doubt they will be coming to our Wakes for gingerbread and ribbons, Thomas," I say, but he does not laugh.

Outside the cave, the beast bellows in the sun. He has squeezed his bulk back through that gape in his desperation to get away from death.

"That beast must be returned," I say.

"Yes, you are right, Samuel." Her voice has music in it, I think. "And you must be the one to take him back. You are the property owner, after all."

This was not the way it was meant to be.

"But what about Thomas!"

"He will stay with me. Thomas will protect me from the ghosts," she says. Thomas still streams and snuffles, but when he hears what she says he sets back his scrawny shoulders and swallows his sobs.

"Come back for Thomas later," she says to me.

Damn him.

Now it is *me* who roars down that sour hillside as I

drive the beast back to the pinfold. My face is awash with sweat and anger. Our poor apprentice, our cheap labour, Thomas Tricklebank, is to be rewarded sitting with the pretty stranger, while *I* struggle to return our beast from the mouth of hell where *Thomas* drove it!

I curse him! *Clackfart, pauper, gormless barmpot.*

I yell how I shall pull off his hair and do violence to his privy members!

Those skeletons sit in my mind. I cannot rid it of their folds of bones, as yellow-white as the keys on a piano I saw once through a rich man's window in Ashbourne town.

I suppose that I must tell the curate of those bones.

Our village lies under a blanket of heat. Everyone is too hot, too slattened, to stay awake. I drive the beast back into the pinfold and the sheep part like a grey sea. I carry water for them all and dunk my face and splash my body in it. Even the bones of Agnes Wood's roasted swine are picked clean. None left for me.

On to the curate's house in Maggot Lane. I knock on the door, doubting that he was watching over his church last night as he is meant to do. For on the eve of Wakes, the sins of the year are cleansed. Women sweep the hay from the church floor. They spread fresh rushes and lavender to make the stone smell sweeter. It banishes bad spirits.

My mother would leave posies of flowers upon the seats, to welcome those who came to church.

I knock again. The door is opened a crack. A pair of mezzled eyes meet mine. This curate has no licence or degree from university. He lives incontinently with a woman whose marriage promise was not kept. I glimpse the paleness of her arms and throat against the painted cloth of his wall.

"There are bones up at Ringinglow Rocks," I tell him.

"A dead ewe in the winter, perhaps..."

"No! We found bones from antiquity."

"We?"

"Myself and Thomas Tricklebank. And the girl..."

"Which girl?"

"That small, brown-skinned girl. She is come to the Wakes."

"Where has she come from?"

I shrug. He is parson. *He* should know.

"Find out where she comes from and send her back again," he grunts. "This village cannot harbour more paupers. We need no more suspicious persons here. Bid her go!"

(The poor may expect little from such a Christian soul as he.)

I bid the peeping parson Good Day and make my way wearily back up the moor to Ringinglow Rocks. I want to show my father my success, but not so much as I want to be back in the cave with the sloe-eyed girl.

She is gone.

Just as Thomas is there, leaning his head against a rock, asleep. His hand clutches a posy of wilting flowers. Above him the bones remain. I see their glimmer in the corner of my eye but I will not turn and face them.

I suppose Thomas sleeps after his fright. I shake his shoulder and say, more kindly than I feel, "Come on, Thomas. We must get back."

He opens his eyes, looks up at me. He does not whimper. He smiles. He clambers to his feet and stretches, then follows me back down the moor-side. Thunder rumbles far away. the light has changed. The sky is bruised with a hot storm to come.

I never found out who she was. Thomas would say nothing of her, only smile. Thomas has left our village.

I heard it said he is to be clerk to a Blue John merchant in Buxton.

Some weeks later, scholars came, summoned by the curate. They were sober and aloof. They took the bones away to learn from them.

I never saw the girl again. Until today. There she sits, sideways, on the white pony, that leads a line of jaggers' ponies, carrying lead ore over the Peak.

She looks straight at me. Her eyes are dark blue-black as sloe-berries.

Quick!...

Angelino's Snowman
Gill Vickery

Assunta turned her back on the window and the snow barging against the glass on its silent way across the piazza. "It's five hundred years since Florence saw snow like this." She poured coffee into three cups set out on a tray.

"Is it?" I said.

"Not only that," her busy hands added milk, sugar and a plate of pastries, "today the planets and the stars are aligned in the same pattern as then."

"What does that mean?" I asked, swallowing the last crumbs of the pastry she'd let me steal.

"It means that something will happen." Her dark eyes were troubled. The something was bad.

"The only thing that's going to happen is that my father's going to be more bad-tempered than usual because he's quarrelling with the other professors and they're winning."

Assunta tutted at such disrespect: she loved me, but she worshipped my father. He does that, inspires worship. He has charisma. Assunta thrust the tray at me. "Take the coffee and try to behave like a well-educated child."

I carried the heavy tray carefully across the big, stone-flagged kitchen and turned to push the door open with my back. Assunta was watching the snow again, whirling and cavorting outside in the piazza. As I backed through the door I saw her eyes close and her mouth move in what I suppose was a prayer, or maybe an invocation, to her favourite saint, Gennaro. My mother is right, the Italians are a superstitious people.

I went up the back stairs of our house, the ones built hundreds of years ago for servants and anyone wanting discreet access to one of the upstairs rooms. This way, I could get into the library via a little carpeted lobby where I could eavesdrop on my father's meeting. When I got there, his loud voice was furious: "Any fool can see they're genuine," he roared.

"Are you calling us all fools?" I recognised the voice of Professor Carbone, the world's second-greatest authority on the artists of the High Renaissance.

"It was a figure of speech." That was the closest to an apology that Father was going to give her. "The drawings are genuine, the paper is genuine, the provenance is indisputable."

Professor Koningsburg joined in: "But the medium is graphite and graphite did not exist in Italy in the fifteenth century — or anywhere else at that time. I admit the drawings are convincing, but the anomaly of the graphite cannot be ignored." The professor's voice was weary. I knew the argument had been going round in circles for a long time. The professors deserved their coffee. I took it into the library, warm and cosy with its coal fire.

"What do you want?" my father snapped.

"I've brought the coffee," I said. I swear I meant to be careful; I meant to behave well, as Assunta warned me to, and I did clamp my mouth shut. Only my hands, shaking the slightest bit, showed that my father's attitude had got to me again. Of course he noticed.

"Be careful, you stupid child!"

That made me shake more and the coffee cups jumped in their tiny saucers, the sugar and milk and the plate of pastries slipped sideways on the tray.

"The drawings!" As he lunged forward, Father's elbow jogged the tray. A cup tipped and coffee slopped

166

onto an angel. We all stared at the drawing — me, my father and the two art experts. Behind me the fire spat in derision.

"Sorry," I said. And I meant it. Fake or not, the drawing had been beautiful.

"Why," my father said, "do you always have to behave like an imbecile?"

I kept a grip on my temper and picked up the cup, intending to put it back on the tray.

"It's too late for that, you little fool," Father said.

So I poured the rest of the coffee over the drawing. "I hate you," I said, and left the library. I couldn't believe what I'd done; ruined, totally ruined, a masterpiece that might be worth thousands, just because I was angry with my father. I walked carefully, I couldn't see clearly through my furious, terrified tears and I didn't want to stumble. "Come back!" my father ordered. I took no notice. I ran down the stairs and slammed into the kitchen. "I hate him! I hate him!"

"What's the matter?" Assunta said. There was no point in telling her: she'd been the family maid since before I was born, she was bound to take his side.

I ran out of the kitchen, the house, across the piazza and down the winding white streets, past the bell tower and the cathedral, its dome veiled in bridal swirls of snow. I ran down more streets, faster and faster until I could scarcely breathe. I stopped and leaned against a wall, up to my knees in the snow, wind-piled against the freezing stone. Now, instead of anger, it was the bone-biting cold that made me shiver. The worst snowfall in Florence since Assunta's legendary winter of 1494 and I was in the middle of it. Snow hurtled silently downwards, blotting out the sky, the roofs, the high walls. A great gust of it came billowing like a giant's sigh from a narrow alleyway. It rolled over me in a cloud, wet and cold. All I could see was whiteness, all I could hear was my breathing and my father calling my name from far away: "Anna! Anna!"

How dare he use that name? Only my mother called me Anna; only she had the right. Was he trying to pretend he was concerned about me? I didn't believe it for a minute. I plunged on into the furious whiteness.

"Anna! Anna, where are you?" His voice was fainter. Why didn't he leave me alone? He didn't want me around. He didn't even like me. I ploughed on in the blinding whiteness. Snow seeped through my clothes like a virus and chilled my skin; even my blood felt like it was slowly freezing in my veins. I stopped and blinked away the ice crystals forming on my lashes. I couldn't control my shivering. Like it or not, I was going to have to go back. But I wasn't going to call for help from my father, there must be some Fiorentini around the streets. "Hello!" The snow muffled my voice like a cold hand. "Hello!" I yelled, as loudly as I could.

"Andrea?" Father was using my proper name now. It meant he'd stopped feeling worried and was just angry with me as usual. I tramped forward, wondering how he'd managed to get ahead of me.

"Andrea!" I wasn't sure now that it was my father's voice, it sounded younger, lighter, and more excited than worried. Before I could make up my mind about that, the cloud whirled away down the alley, leaving me in a place where the air was clear and the snow settled over the street and houses, its millions of crystals winking in the high, pale sun. I knew where I was — on the Via Cavour beside the solid bulk of the Medici Palace. But it was all wrong: there was no traffic, except for a couple of carts and some horses, and the people streaming along to the palace were dressed in fifteenth-century costume, perfect down to the last belt and button. I knew it was perfect because my father and mother had steeped me in Renaissance art and history from the day I was born.

"Andrea!" It was the voice I'd heard through the cold cloud that drew me down the alley. Now I could see it belonged to a boy of about sixteen, flushed with excitement and the cold, but it wasn't me he was calling to, it was another boy across the road. I should've known from the way he pronounced 'Andrea', the boy's way — *An-drey-a* — with the stress on the *drey* instead of the *an* part.

"Is it true, Francesco?" Andrea asked as he reached his friend. "That arrogant stone-cutter brat's been ordered to build a giant snowman?"

"Yes, everyone's going to watch, including me." Francesco knocked Andrea's fancy pancake-shaped hat off. "And he's more than a stone-cutter, which is why you're so jealous."

He hurried into the palace with his friend following, furiously brushing the snow off his hat. I lost sight of them in the growing stream of Fiorentini who jostled me down the road and through the great, iron-banded, wooden doors of the palace. I was too numb with cold and shock to resist. Anyway, where else can I go? I thought, as I was swept down the stone-flagged passageway and into a courtyard filling up with people chattering and exclaiming in a peculiar, throaty Tuscan accent.

I managed to get behind one of the columns supporting the cloisters running all the way round the courtyard and tried not to believe the impossible thing that had happened to me. I made myself go over the evidence in order, step by step, in the process Father had taught me. I'd been lost in a snowstorm; I'd run into the cold cloud, then walked towards someone calling my name. After that, the blinding cloud had left me here, on a bright winter's day, with a settled snowfall over the Via Cavour, which had no cars or scooters running down it. Now I was in the Medici Palace with people all around me wearing fifteenth-century clothes. Then there was the way they spoke. It sounded a bit like the poetry of Dante that Father had made me learn and which was the equivalent of Shakespearean English. It was this last fact, more than anything, which forced me to accept that Assunta's 'something' had happened: I'd gone from one day in 1994 to the exact same time five hundred years before. I tried to remember what I'd learned about time, relativity and the physics of string theory. It wasn't a lot; my home education programmes didn't include much science. I was scared. Renaissance Italy was a cruel and barbaric place. On the other hand, I'd got here so there must be a way back. But how was I going to find it? I had no idea. I leaned on the pillar and tried not to panic. What would my father tell me to do? Stop worrying about events over which I had no control, keep my eyes open for the way back and make the most of this chance to live inside history. I decided the only thing I could do was to stay on the sidelines for now, and observe.

I pulled my jacket tightly round me and crept from the shelter of the pillar into the crowd gathered round the edge of the courtyard. I've been there quite a lot in my time and it didn't seem much different from what I was used to: a square, open, courtyard enclosed by a colonnade of arches with huge stone medallions mounted on the inner walls. There were a few statues that were new to me, though the biggest difference was the gigantic pillar of snow at the far end, heaped up and squared off into a thick, straight-sided column. I worked my way closer till I was next to Francesco and his friend. They were tormenting a skinny, dark-haired boy, standing beside the column of snow sparkling in the sunlight slanting into the courtyard. "Angelino," Francesco called, "this is your greatest commission yet — a snowman!"

His friend joined in: "It will last forever as a testament to your genius." The boy ignored the taunts and the laughter from the crowd, though the red flush on the back of his neck told me he was angry. He'd got more self-control than me. He swung off the heavy violet cloak he was wearing and held it out to Francesco. "Bring me a spade," he said.

It was Francesco's turn to blush. "Oh, I'm your apprentice now, am I?" He bowed and took the cloak. "Maestro." The crowd laughed again and people began to bow or curtsey too. I can't stand being laughed at — it's one of the things Father does when he thinks I've been particularly stupid — and from the way the flush spread up to Angelino's face, neither could he. I forgot about trying to be inconspicuous. I shoved Francesco out of the way and grabbed two spades from the pile of tools propped up against a pillar. "Which one?" I asked Angelino.

He took the larger one. He didn't thank me, only gave me a nod and went straight to work scoring deep lines from top to bottom of the pillar of snow. He had amazing energy for such a slight boy; snow flew over his clothes, his hair, his face, as he chopped with the wooden blade, like a soldier hacking at an enemy. A figure began to emerge from the snow, liberated by the ferocious slicing; a figure in long flowing robes, its head turned toward the sun. Chop - slash - chop - slash. The robes turned to wings poised against the body at the exact moment before spreading wide and lifting in

171

flight. Angelino tossed the spade away, clicked his fingers at me. I gave him the smaller spade. He worked away at the limbs, the planes of the head, the streaming hair, began to cut a suggestion of feathers into the wings, flowing like the liquid the snow once was. The second spade was hurled away. "I need a knife," Angelino said, "and a ladder." Francesco brought both. He wasn't laughing now. Angelino balanced the ladder carefully against the snow statue and went lightly, quickly up to chip and slice the imprisoning snow away from the frozen face. He turned the blade in his hand, touched the point to the blind white eyes and with two deft twists, opened them and let them look out onto the world. The yearning in those cold eyes made me ache with longing for the things I knew I'd never have.

Angelino came down from the ladder and this time Francesco took it away without being asked. Angelino gave him the knife back. The crowd broke into applause and roared its approval. "It's truly an angel of God," Francesco said. Angelino grunted and wiped chunks of melting snow from his hair.

"It looks sad," I said. I was sad too. "He'll melt away when the sun warms up. It'll be as though he never existed."

"Of course," Angelino said.

I understood. "It's not an angel!"

"No."

"It's Icarus."

My mother had told me the story long ago. Icarus and his father were prisoners on an island and his father made them both wings with the feathers held in place by wax. He warned Icarus not to fly too close to the sun, but he forgot.

"He flew too high, the wax melted and he fell into the sea and drowned."

Angelino smiled at me. He was never going to be good-looking, not with his jug ears and his flat, broken nose, but his smile was like a gift. It lit up his strange yellow-brown eyes and it was that light which told me who he really was. I'd read the famous description too often to be mistaken: his friend Giorgio wrote that Angelino's eyes were, 'the colour of horn with yellowish gleams'.

"I envy you," I said, "for what you've done and what you will do."

The eyes gleamed again. "Who are you?" Angelino asked.

"My name's Wyatt, Andrea Wyatt." For once I was glad of my ambiguous name: it didn't conflict with the fact I was wearing trousers, which I knew made everyone think I was a boy. And being foreign might account for my clothes being a bit odd. "I'm a visitor from England. My mother is Italian. My father, he..." I didn't know how to describe him; there weren't any art historians in the fifteenth century. "He's a scholar." That was true. "He's searching for paintings and sculptures to take back to England." That was true as well, sort of. Now I'd got the knack of telling almost-truths, I plunged on recklessly. "He's heard of how promising your work is and is eager to learn more."

The crowd pressed in, impatient that I was monopolising Angelino. They wanted to congratulate him on his angel. Francesco shouldered me aside to drape the violet cloak over Angelino. "I'm not cold," he said and shrugged it off.

"I meant it to cover you," Francesco said. "The Prince is coming to inspect your snowman." He nodded up at the balcony running around the courtyard, where a couple of servants were opening a door. He tried again to cloak Angelino's black clothes stained with sweat and

173

melted snow. "You look like a workman."

"To him I am a workman."

Angelino gave the cloak to me. "You're cold. Go to my rooms. You can get warm there and we'll talk about your father. Francesco will show you the way."

"I want to see the Prince," Francesco objected.

"Then you'd better hurry."

Francesco gave in. He led me at a run through the palace and up wide stone stairs, along back corridors and through doors until we came to a large room carpeted in scarlet and with a fire burning steadily in the grate. It made me think of the one in my father's library. I wondered if it had burned out or if Assunta had built it up. Ragged cheering and uneven clapping came filtering through the cloth shutter over the window.

"The Prince!" Francesco left quickly.

I lifted the shutter. On a balcony overlooking the courtyard, a man stood in the middle of a group of lords and ladies in bright brocades and silks and velvets. He peered down his long nose at Icarus and at Angelino, who was the only person in the crowd whose head wasn't lowered. "I didn't want an angel," the man said, "I wanted a grotesque."

Angelino shrugged the tiniest bit. One of the ladies whispered in the man's ear. "The Principessa tells me the angel is very beautiful, nevertheless," he said.

"Then I thank the Principessa." Angelino bowed to her.

The crowd held its breath at the insult, and so did I. Angelino was playing a dangerous game. This was 1494 and I knew that meant the man was Piero de' Medici, 'prince' and ruler of Florence. It didn't matter that Angelino had been a favourite of Piero's father, had grown up with Piero, eaten at the same table, been

174

taught alongside him by the most famous scholars of the age: Piero was weak, rich and arrogant. The people of Florence lived and died on his uncertain word. He looked at Icarus again. "It is indeed a very beautiful angel," he said. "But next time you will make a grotesque." He held out his hand and a servant put a little bag in it. He threw it down to Angelino who caught it and bowed. He kept his head down until Piero and his party moved back into the palace. As the doors closed behind them, he straightened and hefted the pouch. In the clear air, I heard it jingle.

The crowd broke up, some taking a closer look at the snowman, some leaving, some like Angelino and his friends going into the palace. I took out my sketchbook and the tin of pencils that go everywhere with me. I draw all the time. It's one of the things Father approved of, though he disparaged my skills. I leaned on the broad window ledge and drew Icarus. It was difficult, the perspective was acute from this high up and no matter how I tried I couldn't get it right. How Father would enjoy that. I could hear his voice in my mind: "Perspective is only a technique, a basic skill, simple enough." I blew on my hands, my sigh of frustration turning to a cloud of frosty breath.

"That's good," a voice said. How long had Angelino been there watching me try to draw? He took my book and studied the picture, then drew a few eloquent lines with my pencil. They transformed my sketch. "You see?" he said.

"Yes."

He showed me more, exploring the wings, the face, the twists and turns of the body — every line, every mark defining a longing for freedom. He thrust the book back at me.

"Thank you," I said.

175

He took no notice, he was too busy turning the pencil over and over, running his rough fingers across the black and red surface, reading the white lettering. Abruptly he said, "Sit!" I dropped into a chair under the window where the pure, cold light streamed through.

Angelino snatched up a thick sheet of paper, pushed aside the saffron and blue crockery littering a table and began to draw, his strange, fierce eyes flickering from me to the paper and back again. I didn't dare to move or speak. I fixed my attention on a little shrine hanging on the opposite wall, its gilded doors shining with a buttery gleam from the votive lamp flickering and smoking in front of it. I'm not religious, despite my mother's efforts, but I thought it wouldn't do any harm to try praying for guidance on getting home, especially as the saint kneeling in front of the Madonna and Child was Assunta's favourite, Gennaro. My stomach rumbled. It was a long time since I'd eaten Assunta's pastry.

I wasn't any good at praying. All I could think of was getting home. I forced myself to concentrate on the painting, trying to assess it in the way Father had taught me. It was very old, old even in Angelino's time. The rules of painting were different then: Mary and her baby were bigger than the saint because they were more important than him. The artist was telling you to concentrate on them. The background was plain gold to show how precious the picture was, and the Madonna's gown was painted in the most expensive blue made from lapis lazuli.

Concentrating on the picture didn't stop my muscles getting stiff as the pleats in its sharply painted folds of drapery. How long had I sat here? Long enough for the tiny lamp to burn down and fill the air with a thick smell of hot oil.

Angelino gave a little grunt of what sounded like satisfaction and stopped drawing. He held the pencil out to me, reluctantly. "Keep it," I said.

"Then you have this." He gave me the drawing.

It was me, yet not me. The face was my face, yet beautiful; my face, yet a boy's face; my face, yet seen through the eyes of the past. It was exquisite and it told me I had no business being here.

"It's wonderful," I said.

"Show it to your father. If he likes it he might commission work from me to take back to England."

I thought of Father and took a risk. "You have to sign it, so he truly knows which artist did it."

I knew that in all his long life, Angelino never signed his work, except for once. But he wrote his name on his picture of me. As he wrote, the light falling on the paper turned from pale gold to blue white.

"It's snowing!" I slid the drawing into my book and ran out of the room, out of the palace and into the courtyard.

Angelino followed me. "Wait!"

"I can't." I'd arrived in a blizzard, it stood to reason I had to leave in one. I flew past Icarus, down the stone passageway and into the road. The cloud billowed from the alleyway.

"What's that?" Angelino was beside me.

"My way home." I unwound the cloak and shook off the snow settling like ermine along its shoulders and gave it back to Angelino.

"Here." He took a coin from the pouch Piero had thrown to him and put it in my hand. A golden florin.

"Why?"

"Because you helped me with Icarus and asked no questions."

I took my precious tin of pencils, a present from my

mother to help pass the time during the access visit to Father. "This is for you."

I ran into the roiling whiteness. "Adio, Angelino!" I shouted without looking back. I felt my way blindly forward, groping at the freezing air, on and on, step by step. What if I wasn't going forwards at all? What if I went round and round forever, trapped between then and now? I wanted to go home. I wanted my present, my future. "Father!" I shouted.

"Anna? Anna, where are you?"

"I'm here." I stumbled numbly towards my father's voice. In one step, I was out in the road, the white cloud boiling backwards down the alley behind me. My father stood in the moonlit street, his arms wide. "Anna!"

"I got lost," I wailed.

Father wrapped me up in his coat and scarf and hat and helped me pull gloves over my frozen hands: there was no lecture, Father only said, "Let's go home." We walked back to the house through the snow, the moonlight silver-plating the city.

I didn't ask how long I'd been missing, not till after I'd had a bath to warm up and Assunta had brought me dinner in bed while my father rang the Polizia to tell them I was back. I'd been gone for twelve hours. Time had passed much faster inside the cloud, as it moved me through the five hundred years.

"I didn't mean to cause trouble," I said to Assunta, who'd stayed to look after me.

"You never do," she said, collecting my tray of empty dishes. "You are a foolish and stubborn child," she scolded. "And your father is a foolish and stubborn man. You should have talked long ago. Now would be a good time to start, while you are both ashamed of yourselves and willing to listen to each other."

She was right. Father and I talked for a long time and

178

it was a new beginning. It was only when there was nothing left to say of our past history, that Father asked me where I'd been after I ran away from the house. I'd already thought about how to tell him. I was going to give the facts and nothing else, and let Father work it out to his own satisfaction.

"I got into the Medici Palace courtyard. A boy about my age, you'd call him a youth, was building a snowman, more of a snow sculpture really, and I stopped to help. He paid me." I held out the florin. While Father examined the five-hundred-year-old, newly minted, gold coin, I opened my sketchbook. "This is the snowman he made."

"You did this drawing?"

"Yes. And Angelino — that was the boy's name — corrected it. Then he drew these other studies. People came to laugh at him because he was an artist who'd been ordered to make a snowman but he decided to make a work of art, even though the sun would melt it. They thought he'd made an angel but I worked out it was Icarus because he was destroyed by the sun too."

I tweaked my portrait from the book and gave the sheet to my father. "Later, Angelino drew me. I asked him to sign the drawing and he did. Look, at the bottom."

Father studied it for a long time. I had no idea what he was thinking. At last he said, "Anna, tell me *everything* that happened."

It took a long time as he interrupted me over and over again with questions. Before, I'd have lost my temper and told him to leave me alone, but now I understood it was his way, it was nothing personal. In the end he stopped and said he was sorry, he'd forgotten how tired I must be.

"You do believe me?"

"Of course, you couldn't possibly have invented that mass of impeccable detail. And don't forget, I'm the world's greatest authority on this artist's work." I think he was teasing me.

"You're not the world's greatest authority on me."

"I'm getting there."

"At least you know you were right about the graphite drawings. Angelino must've done them with my pencils." I shouldn't have mentioned it — we both remembered the coffee incident. "I'm sorry about the angel drawing, Dad, especially now. Is it ruined?"

"I'm afraid it is. Let's forget it. My real regret is that I'll never be able to prove to my colleagues that I was right all along."

I understood how hard that was for him, academics are proud of their reputations. "*I* know you're right. That makes two of us."

He nodded. I wasn't sure it was enough for him.

"Dad." I liked being this informal.

"Anna."

"The drawing of me isn't the angel I ruined, but — would you like it?"

He didn't protest or say, "Are you sure?" Only, "Thank you."

He loved that drawing. He had it framed and hung it near his desk in the library. That was ten years ago. I'm looking at the picture now as I wait for Dad to take me out to dinner to celebrate the opening of my first solo exhibition in Florence. He would still rather I was a scholar, like him, but he's learned to live with it. I never forgot my drawing lesson with Angelino or his determination to make even a snowman a work of art. Stubbornness can be a positive thing when you don't allow it to blind you to other possibilities.

I smile as I look at Angelino's signature on my

portrait. Of course he didn't sign it 'Angelino' — that was only his nickname, as mine's Anna. He signed it with his proper name: Michelangelo Buonarotti. Michelangelo. According to my father, the greatest artist who ever lived and I've never quarrelled with him about that.

The Writers

David Belbin's novels for Young Adults include *Denial, Love Lessons* and *Dead Guilty* (published by Five Leaves). He works part-time at Nottingham Trent University, where he runs the MA in Creative Writing. *Waking Early, West Kirby*, first appeared in *Lanterns: an anthology of new writing* (2005).
www.davidbelbin.com

Pauline Chandler lives with her family in rural Derbyshire, in a Victorian gasworks. Her latest book, for which, as a work in progress, she was awarded an Arts Council Award in 2003, is *Warrior Girl*, a novel about Joan of Arc.
www.paulinechandler.com

Chris d'Lacey has published twenty-three books for children of varying ages. His first novel, *Fly, Cherokee, Fly* was highly commended for the Carnegie Medal. He is a regular visitor to schools, libraries and festivals. *Fire Star*, the third book in his popular dragon series, is available now.
www.icefire.co.uk

Berlie Doherty has written nearly fifty books and is translated into twenty-one languages. Her books and plays have won many awards, including the Carnegie Medal twice. She has also written libretti for two children's operas. Her most recent titles are *Deep Secret, The Starburster* and *Jinnie Ghost*, a picture book illustrated by Jane Ray.
www.berliedoherty.com

Rowena Edlin-White writes children's fiction and adult non-fiction and has taught writing for children at university level. Previous anthologies include *Dancing on Mountains: an anthology of women's spiritual writings*. Her latest book is *Grace's Diary*, the 19th century journal of a Nottingham school teacher, which she has edited.

Gwen Grant's story is set in the 1950s in a Nottinghamshire pit town. A published poet, her stories and books, ranging from picture books to young adults, have been short-listed for many awards and translated into many languages. She has also won the Acorn Award for Picture Books.
www.gwengrant.co.uk

Sylvia Hall loves to cook, dance, sing, play tennis and walk the Derbyshire hills with her dog, Denver. She writes teen fiction for Scholastic (check out *No Fear* and *Knife Edge*). An English and Drama teacher, she also writes and directs plays for young people.

Linda Kempton is an award-winning author of several books for children, including *The Naming of William Rutherford*, which was nominated for the Carnegie Medal. Writing has brought her many interesting jobs, the most exciting of which was a tour of Jamaica for East Midlands Arts. She lives in Derbyshire.

B. K. Mahal was born and raised in Derby where she lives with her family. After leaving University she wrote her first novel, *The Pocket Guide to Being an Indian Girl*. The extract in this anthology is part of the sequel. During her job as a primary school teacher, she has worked as a consultant for Collins English Dictionaries on Hinglish.

Nick Manns taught English in comprehensive schools for about 100 years, but eventually slipped out of the classroom, looked around, and started tapping away on a computer. He writes books to entertain, to scare, and to raise the kind of questions he'd like answered. The book he enjoyed writing most was *Fallout*.

Lynne Markham was born and brought up in Nottingham, and apart from a few years in Botswana with the National Library Service, has always lived there. Reviewing other writers' work made her want to have a go herself and *Now You See Me* followed. She has published books for a broad spectrum of readers, including *Getting It Right*, *Deep Trouble* and *Blazing Star*.
lynne.pyburn@freeuk.com

Bette Paul is the author of some twenty books ranging from easy readers to long novels for Young Adults, with junior fiction in between, including some of the ubiquitous *Animal Ark* series. Always curious about family relationships, as a child her dream was to lift the roofs off houses in her street and watch how other people lived. Which is, after all, what a writer does, if only in her mind!

Caroline Pitcher's inspiration for *Wakes*, as well as for full-length novels *Mine* and *Silkscreen*, is the landscape of Derbyshire. She has had over fifty books published and has won several awards, including the Arts Council Writers' Award. Her latest novels are *Cloud Cat* and *Sky Shifter*.
www.carolinepitcher.co.uk

Gill Vickery won the Fidler First Novel Award in 2000 for *The Ivy Crown*. *Angelino's Snowman* reflects her interest in painting (especially graphic novels) which she studied for six years at the Joseph Wright School of Art in Derby and then in Cardiff. She lives in Leicestershire.